101 BURGERS & SLIDERS

HAWAIIAN TERIYAKI PORK BURGER
SEE PAGE 93

101
BURGERS
& SLIDERS

CLASSIC AND GOURMET RECIPES FOR
THE MOST POPULAR FAST FOOD

RYLAND PETERS & SMALL
LONDON • NEW YORK

First published in 2017 by
Ryland Peters & Small
20–21 Jockey's Fields
London WC1R 4BW
and
341 E 116th St
New York, NY 10029
www.rylandpeters.com

Recipe collection compiled by
Alice Sambrook. Recipe
text © Amy Ruth Finegold,
Carol Hilker, Dan May, Dunja
Gulin, Jenny Linford, Jordan
Bourke, Louise Pickford, Nicola
Graimes, Mat Follas, Miranda
Ballard, Rachael Anne Hill,
Shelagh Ryan and Ryland
Peters & Small.

Design & photography
© Ryland Peters & Small 2017

A CIP catalog record for this
book is available from the
Library of Congress and the
British Library.

ISBN: 978-1-84975-855-0

Printed in China

10 9 8 7 6 5 4 3 2 1

Editor: Alice Sambrook
Designer: Paul Stradling
Production: David Hearn
Editorial Director: Julia Charles
Art Director: Leslie Harrington
Publisher: Cindy Richards

Indexer: Vanessa Bird

NOTES

• Both British (metric) and
American (imperial plus US
cup) measurements are included;
however, its important not to
alternate between the two within
a recipe.

• All eggs are medium (UK)
or large (US), unless otherwise
specified. It is recommended
that free-range, organic eggs be
used whenever possible. Recipes
containing raw or partially
cooked egg should not be served
to the very young, very old,
anyone with a compromised
immune system or pregnant
women.

• When a recipe calls for grated
zest of citrus fruit, buy unwaxed
fruit and wash well before use.
If you can only find treated fruit,
scrub and rinse before using.

• Ovens should be preheated to
the specified temperatures. All
ovens work slightly differently.
We recommend using an oven
thermometer and suggest you
consult the maker's handbook
for any special instructions,
particularly if you are cooking
in a fan-assisted/convection
oven, as you may need to adjust
temperatures.

CONTENTS

INTRODUCTION

All hail the iconic symbol of fast-food culture, the frequently requested family treat, the ultimate fix for a hungry hangover or a bad day at work: the burger. Once solely a delicious yet formulaic American staple, now burgers are loved around the world in many different cultures and in many different forms. They are most often served as a large satisfying meal, but smaller mini burgers – known as sliders – are just as delicious and make great party food. Clearly, the world has gone crazy for burgers and sliders, and you can find all manner of gourmet varieties in restaurants and food trucks. The flavour combinations are endless...and the range of veggie burger options has also reached new heights.

Armed with this book, you don't need to trek out to an overpriced burger joint when you can quickly and easily whip up something just as good at home. The first chapter, *Simply Delicious*, offers easy-to-make recipes for all-time favourite treats: try the Classic Beefburger with Tomato Ketchup and Lettuce or the Chicken Burger with Herb Mayo. Turn up the heat in the second chapter, *Spice up your Life*, with tasty inventions such as the Buffalo Cauliflower Burger with Blue Cheese Sauce or the Spicy Beef & Pork Sliders with Ginger & Lime. Next up, try something new in *Flavours of the World* with Japanese Salmon Katsu Sliders or Chinese Crispy Duck Sliders with Hoisin & Spring Onion/Scallion. In the next chapter, *Party-time Patties*, discover burgers and sliders for entertaining, such as Christmas Canapé Sliders with Cranberry Sauce & Camembert or fun 'Sausage' Burgers for Kids. *Meat-free Treats* provides a glorious selection of vegetarian burgers – sample the Sticky Sweet Chilli/Chile Halloumi Sliders with Crispy Onion Rings or the Middle Eastern Aubergine/Eggplant Sliders with Tahini Sauce. Indulge in a *Dirty Burger* such as the Deep-fried Buttermilk Chicken Burger with 'Nduja & Slaw or the Triple Whammy Brunch Burger. Treat your sophisticated friends with some *Posh Patties* such as Cajun Salmon, Dill & Crème Fraîche Sliders or a Pork & Antipasti Burger with Lemon Mayo. Finally, take a peek at the *Side Orders* chapter and choose your perfect accompaniment, from Sweet Potato Wedges to Classic Coleslaw and of course a whole range of delicious dips.

Whether you are after a mean meaty tower or a light and delicious vegan number, you can find your perfect patty right here in these pages. Serve the simple recipes as weeknight dinners, slinky sliders are perfect for entertaining friends, and you could even use a gourmet recipe to woo someone special... after all, the ability to make a great burger says a lot about a person!

CLASSIC BEEF BURGER
with tomato ketchup & lettuce

- -

220 g/8 oz. lean minced/ground beef

2 teaspoons tomato purée/paste

1½ tablespoons fresh breadcrumbs

1 teaspoon chopped fresh parsley

1 tablespoon olive or vegetable oil

a large pinch of sea salt and freshly ground black pepper

to serve

2 sesame seed burger buns

Homemade Tomato Ketchup (see page 127)

a few lettuce leaves

serves 2

SOMETIMES LESS IS MORE AND A SIMPLE BURGER MADE WITH GOOD-QUALITY BEEF SPEAKS FOR ITSELF. IT'S WORTH MAKING A BATCH OF HOMEMADE TOMATO KETCHUP TO SERVE WITH THESE BURGERS – IT'S SO MUCH TASTIER THAN ANY STORE-BOUGHT VARIETY.

★ Put the beef in a bowl with the tomato purée/paste, breadcrumbs, parsley and salt and pepper. Work together with your hands until evenly mixed. Divide the beef mixture in half and shape into two burger patties. Press each burger down to make them nice and flat.

★ Heat the oil in a frying pan/skillet and fry the burgers over medium-high heat for 5 minutes on each side until cooked through.

★ Slice the burger buns in half. Spread a spoonful of Homemade Tomato Ketchup on the base of each bun and put the cooked burgers on top. Put a few lettuce leaves on top of each burger and finish with the lids of the buns. Serve at once.

CLASSIC ALL-AMERICAN HAMBURGER

750 g/1½ lb. chuck steak, minced/ground

1 onion, finely chopped

1 teaspoon Worcestershire sauce

sea salt and freshly ground black pepper

olive oil, for brushing

to serve

4 sesame seed buns, halved

2 tablespoons American mustard

a handful of lettuce leaves, shredded

2 tomatoes, sliced

2 dill pickles, sliced

serves 4

FOR A BURGER TO BE TRULY 'ALL-AMERICAN' IT MUST BE SERVED IN A BUN WITH LETTUCE, TOMATO, AMERICAN MUSTARD AND DILL PICKLES, WITH FRENCH FRIES ON THE SIDE.

★ Put the beef, onion, Worcestershire sauce and some salt and pepper in a bowl and work together with your hands until evenly mixed. Divide the mixture into four portions and shape into burger patties. Press each burger down to make them nice and flat. Cover and chill for 30 minutes.

★ Brush the patties lightly with olive oil and barbecue or grill/broil for 4–5 minutes on each side until lightly charred and just cooked through inside.

★ Meanwhile, lightly toast the buns under the grill/broiler or in the toaster. Spread one half of each with mustard. Add the shredded lettuce, patties, tomato slices and dill pickles, squeeze over a little extra mustard and add the bun tops. Serve at once.

CLASSIC CHEESEBURGER

THIS VERSION OF A CHEESEBURGER IS MADE USING A GOOD-QUALITY CHEESE CUT INTO SLICES RATHER THAN THE PROCESSED CHEESE OFTEN USED. YOU CAN VARY THE CHEESE – FOR SOMETHING A LITTLE DIFFERENT, TRY CAMEMBERT OR CRUMBLED ROQUEFORT.

750 g/1½ lb. chuck steak, minced/ground

1 onion, finely chopped

1 garlic clove, crushed

2 teaspoons chopped fresh thyme

olive oil, for brushing

to serve

125 g/4 oz. Cheddar cheese, sliced

4 burger buns, halved

4 tablespoons Classic Mayo (see page 128)

4 large leaves of butter lettuce

2 tomatoes, sliced

½ red onion, thinly sliced

sea salt and freshly ground black pepper

serves 4

★ Put the beef, onion, garlic, thyme and some salt and pepper in a bowl and work together with your hands until evenly mixed and slightly sticky. Divide into four portions and shape into burger patties. Press each burger patty down to make them nice and flat. Cover and chill for 30 minutes.

★ Brush the patties lightly with olive oil and barbecue or grill/broil for 5 minutes on each side until lightly charred and cooked through. Top the patties with the cheese slices and set under a hot grill/broiler for 30 seconds until the cheese has melted. Keep them warm.

★ Lightly toast the buns, under the grill/broiler or in the toaster, then spread each base and top with Classic Mayo. Add the lettuce leaves, cheese-topped patties and tomato and red onion slices. Add the bun tops and serve at once.

CHICKEN STEAK & BACON BURGER with Caesar dressing

CAESAR SALAD IS AS MUCH AN AMERICAN ICON AS A BURGER AND HERE THE TWO COMBINE PERFECTLY IN A GREAT SOURDOUGH SANDWICH. YOU CAN ADD A POACHED EGG TO THE FILLING, IF YOU LIKE.

4 small skinless boneless chicken breasts

4 slices smoked back bacon

8 slices sourdough bread

1 cos/romaine lettuce heart, leaves separated

25 g/1 oz. Parmesan cheese, pared into shavings

sea salt and freshly ground black pepper

olive oil, for brushing

Caesar dressing

4 tablespoons Classic Mayo (see page 128)

4 anchovies in oil, drained and finely chopped

1 garlic clove, crushed

1 teaspoon Worcestershire sauce

1 teaspoon white wine vinegar

½ teaspoon Dijon mustard

serves 4

★ Lay the chicken breast fillets flat on a chopping board and, using a sharp knife, cut horizontally through the thickest part but don't cut all the way through. Open the fillets out flat. Brush with olive oil and season with salt and pepper.

★ Preheat a ridged stovetop grill pan until hot and cook the chicken fillets for 3–4 minutes on each side until cooked through. Keep them warm.

★ Cook the bacon on the hot grill pan for 2–3 minutes until cooked to your liking. Keep it warm.

★ Toast the sourdough on the grill pan until lightly charred.

★ Meanwhile, to make the dressing, put the Classic Mayo, anchovies, garlic, Worcestershire sauce, vinegar and mustard in a bowl and beat well. Add salt and pepper to taste.

★ Spread each slice of sourdough with a little Caesar dressing and top half of them with lettuce, chicken, bacon and Parmesan shavings. Finish with a second slice of sourdough and serve at once.

CHICKEN BURGER
with herb mayonnaise

750 g/1½ lb. skinless boneless chicken breasts, minced/ground

1 tablespoon milk

1 small onion, finely chopped

2 garlic cloves, crushed

sea salt and freshly ground black pepper

olive oil, for brushing

to serve

4 sesame seed buns, halved

4 tablespoons Herb Mayo (see page 129), plus extra to serve

a handful of baby spinach leaves

2 tomatoes, sliced

serves 4

CHICKEN MAKES A LIGHTER BURGER THAN MEAT DOES BUT IS NO LESS DELICIOUS. DON'T OVERWORK THE MIXTURE AS YOU PROCESS IT – USE THE PULSE BUTTON AND BLEND BRIEFLY, CHECKING THE MIXTURE EACH TIME BEFORE PROCESSING AGAIN.

★ Put the chicken, milk, onion, garlic and some salt and pepper in a food processor and pulse until smooth. Transfer the mixture to a bowl, cover and chill for 30 minutes.

★ Divide the mixture into four portions and, using wet hands, shape into burger patties. Press each burger down to make them nice and flat. Brush the patties lightly with olive oil and barbecue or grill/broil for 5–6 minutes on each side until cooked through. Test one by inserting a metal skewer into the centre – it should feel hot to the touch when the patty is cooked. Keep them warm.

★ Lightly toast the buns under the grill/broiler or in the toaster and spread the top halves with Herb Mayo. Fill the buns with spinach leaves, patties and tomato slices and serve with extra herb mayo.

180 g/6 oz. lean minced/ground lamb

30 g/¼ cup chopped feta

½ finely chopped red onion

4 pitted black olives, chopped

1 garlic clove, finely chopped

3 tablespoons fresh breadcrumbs

a pinch of ground cumin

2 teaspoons tomato purée/paste

a pinch of sea salt and freshly ground black pepper

tzatziki

200 g/¾ cup plain yogurt

12-cm/5-in. piece of cucumber, peeled and coarsely grated

1 garlic clove, crushed

1 tablespoon extra virgin olive oil

½ teaspoon red wine vinegar

1 tablespoon finely chopped fresh mint

sea salt

to serve

2 pita breads

a handful of baby spinach leaves

2 cooked beetroot/beets, grated

serves 2

LAMB & FETA BURGER
with tzatziki, baby spinach & beetroot/beets

THIS GREEK-STYLE BURGER IS SO TASTY AND VERY EASY TO PREPARE, MAKING IT PERFECT FOR A FAMILY DINNER ON A WARM EVENING. THE HOMEMADE TZATZIKI ADDS A DELICIOUS TOUCH OF AUTHENTICITY TO THIS DISH.

★ To make the tzatziki, put the yogurt in a bowl with the cucumber. Add the garlic, olive oil, vinegar, mint and salt, to taste. Mix well with a fork. Cover with clingfilm/plastic wrap and leave to chill in the fridge.

★ To make the burgers, put the lamb in a bowl with the feta, onion, olives, garlic, breadcrumbs, cumin, tomato purée/paste and salt and pepper. Work together with your hands until evenly mixed. Divide the mixture in half and shape into two burger patties. Press each burger down to make them nice and flat.

★ Lay the burgers on a baking sheet and grill/broil for 5 minutes on each side until cooked through.

★ Cut each of the pitas down one side, to make an opening. Heat a ridged stovetop grill pan to hot. Put the pitas face down in the pan and turn over after about 30 seconds to brown the other side. Alternatively, toast lightly in the toaster, taking care not to let them fully toast and crack.

★ Spread some tzatziki inside each of the warm pitas. Put the cooked burgers inside with a few baby spinach leaves and serve with a spoonful of grated beetroot/beets and baby spinach leaves on the side, if liked.

BACON BURGER with sour cream slaw

625 g/1¼ lb. minced/ground beef

125 g/4 oz. smoked back bacon, minced/ground

1 onion, finely chopped

1 garlic clove, crushed

1 tablespoon freshly chopped sage leaves

1 egg yolk

1 tablespoon wholegrain mustard

sea salt and freshly ground black pepper

olive oil, for brushing

to serve

4 poppy seed rolls, halved

4 iceberg lettuce leaves

2 tomatoes, sliced

½ recipe Sour Cream Slaw (see page 131)

serves 4

SMOKED BACON ADDS GREAT FLAVOUR TO THESE PATTIES, WHICH ARE EQUALLY GOOD MADE FROM MINCED CHICKEN. SOUR CREAM SLAW MAKES A CHANGE FROM REGULAR CLASSIC COLESLAW.

★ Put the beef, bacon, onion, garlic, sage, egg yolk, mustard and some salt and pepper in a bowl and work together with your hands to form a slightly sticky mixture. Divide into four portions and shape into burger patties. Press each burger down to make them nice and flat. Cover and chill for 30 minutes.

★ Brush the patties lightly with olive oil and barbecue or grill/broil for 5 minutes on each side until cooked through. Keep them warm.

★ Lightly toast the poppy seed rolls under the grill/broiler or in the toaster and fill them with lettuce leaves, tomato slices, the patties and the Sour Cream Slaw. Serve at once.

HEALTHY COD BURGER with watercress & almond pesto

LIGHTLY SALTING THE COD BEFORE COOKING FIRMS UP THE FLESH, MAKING IT EASIER TO FRY AND HOLD TOGETHER, AND THUS MORE SUITABLE FOR A BURGER. PAIRED WITH A SIMPLE WATERCRESS PESTO, IT'S HARD TO BELIEVE THIS IS A HEALTHY DISH!

4 x 150 g/6 oz. cod fillets

2 teaspoons sea salt

1 tablespoon olive oil

grated zest of 1 lemon

4 sprigs thyme, leaves picked

salt and freshly ground black pepper

watercress & almond pesto

25 g/1 oz. blanched almonds

100 g/2 cups watercress leaves

juice of 1 lemon

1 garlic clove, crushed

2 tablespoons basil leaves

2 tablespoons natural yogurt

1 tablespoon extra virgin olive oil

to serve

4 seeded rolls

125 g/4 oz. baby plum tomatoes, halved

serves 4

★ Trim the cod fillets and remove any remaining bones. Place in a shallow bowl and add the salt, rubbing it lightly into the fish, then set aside for 2 hours. Rinse the fish under cold water and pat dry using paper towels.

★ Combine the oil with the lemon zest, thyme leaves and some salt and pepper. Rub into the fish and set aside until required.

★ Make the pesto. Dry fry the almonds in a small frying pan/skillet until lightly browned. Roughly chop half the watercress and place in the food processor with the almonds, lemon juice, garlic, basil, yogurt, oil from the burgers and a little salt and pepper. Blend until fairly smooth.

★ Heat a frying pan/skillet over a medium heat and fry the cod fillets for 2–3 minutes on each side until golden. Rest for 3 minutes.

★ Cut the rolls in half and lightly toast the cut sides under the grill/broiler. Place a fish fillet onto each base and spoon over the pesto, then add the remaining watercress leaves and the halved tomatoes. Serve at once.

FISH BURGER
with capers & tartare sauce

250 g/9 oz. boned salmon fillets

50 g/2 oz. cooked small prawns/shrimp

30 g/⅓ cup fresh breadcrumbs

1 tablespoon beaten egg

1 tablespoon capers, chopped

1 garlic clove, finely chopped

1 teaspoon finely grated Parmesan cheese

a good pinch of freshly chopped chives

a good pinch of freshly chopped parsley

a pinch of sea salt and freshly ground black pepper

to serve

2 sesame or plain bagels

tartare sauce

a handful of baby spinach leaves

Classic Homecut Fries (see page 125)

serves 2

THIS SALMON AND PRAWN/SHRIMP BURGER IS A REAL TREAT FOR ANYONE WHO ENJOYS A BURGER BUT DOESN'T WANT TO EAT MEAT. SERVE WITH CLASSIC HOMECUT FRIES FOR A HEARTY MEAL.

★ Preheat the oven to 180°C (350°F) Gas 4.

★ Put the salmon fillets in a greased baking dish and bake for 20 minutes, turning halfway through cooking. Remove from the oven and set aside until cool enough to handle. Leave the oven on.

★ Put the prawns/shrimp in a bowl with the breadcrumbs, egg, capers, garlic, Parmesan, chives, parsley and salt and pepper. Work together with your hands until evenly mixed. Remove the skin from the salmon and break it up into flakes, add to the bowl and mix again. Divide the mixture in half and shape into two burger patties. Press each burger down to make them nice and flat.

★ Lay the burgers on a baking sheet and bake in the preheated oven for 15–20 minutes, turning halfway through cooking.

★ Slice each bagel in half and lightly toast them under the grill/broiler or in the toaster. Spread the bottom half of each bagel with tartare sauce. Put a cooked burger on top and cover with a few baby spinach leaves. Finish the burgers with the lids of the bagels and serve with Classic Homecut Fries.

SPICY BEEF & PORK SLIDERS with ginger & lime

100 g/3½ oz. lean minced/ground beef

100 g/3½ oz. lean minced/ground pork

1 fresh red or green chilli/chile, finely chopped

1 tablespoon freshly squeezed lime juice

½ teaspoon ground ginger

3 tablespoons fresh breadcrumbs

1 tablespoon olive or vegetable oil

a pinch of sea salt and freshly ground black pepper

to serve

6 chicory/Belgian endive leaves

2 fresh red chillies/chiles, deseeded and finely sliced

2 spring onions/scallions, finely sliced

6 cocktail sticks/toothpicks (optional)

makes 6

THESE PUNCHY ASIAN-STYLE SLIDERS ARE IDEAL FOR EATING OUTDOORS ON A WARM SUMMER'S EVENING. THE LIME AND GINGER SOAK PERFECTLY INTO THE MEAT AND A TOUCH OF SPICE ADDS A WELCOME KICK TO EVERY MOUTHFUL.

★ Put the beef and pork in a bowl with the chilli/chile, lime juice, ginger, breadcrumbs and salt and pepper. Work together with your hands until evenly mixed. Divide the beef mixture into six equal portions and shape into six slider patties. Press each slider down to make them nice and flat.

★ Heat the oil in a frying pan/skillet and fry the sliders over a medium–high heat for 3 minutes on each side until cooked through.

★ Put the chicory/Belgian endive leaves face up on a serving plate. Put a slider on top of each leaf, top with chilli/chile and spring onions/scallions. Put a cocktail stick/toothpick through the middle of each slider to hold them together, if liked, and serve at once.

BUFFALO CAULIFLOWER BURGER

with blue cheese sauce

----

75 g/½ cup gram/chickpea flour
or plain/all-purpose flour

1 teaspoon mustard powder

1 teaspoon ground cumin

1 teaspoon smoked paprika

120 ml/½ cup whole milk

florets from one cauliflower,
about 500 g/1 lb. 2 oz.

2 tablespoons chilli/chile sauce

1 tablespoon clear honey

1 tablespoon butter

salt and freshly ground black
pepper

blue cheese dressing

4 tablespoons sour cream

50 g/2 oz. creamy blue cheese

1 tablespoon white wine vinegar

1 tablespoon freshly chopped
chives

½ teaspoon caster/granulated
sugar

salt and freshly ground black
pepper

to serve

4 burger buns

6–8 leaves iceberg lettuce

serves 4

A CLASSIC AMERICAN CHICKEN WING DISH GIVEN THE VEGGIE TREATMENT WITH ROAST CAULIFLOWER FLORETS REPLACING THE CHICKEN. SERVED WITH A CREAMY BLUE CHEESE SAUCE, THIS IS FINGER-LICKING GOOD.

★ Preheat the oven to 220°C (425°F) Gas 7 and line a baking sheet with baking parchment.

★ In a bowl, combine the flour, mustard powder, cumin, paprika and a little salt and pepper. Gradually whisk in the milk with 50 ml/3½ tablespoons cold water until the batter is smooth.

★ Dip each cauliflower floret into the batter and then shake off the excess so the cauliflower is just very lightly coated. Place on the prepared baking sheet, leaving space in between each floret. Roast in the preheated oven for 20 minutes.

★ Warm together the chilli/chile sauce, honey and butter in a small saucepan over a low heat until combined. Remove the cauliflower from the oven, drizzle over the warm sauce and stir well until evenly coated. Return to the oven for a further 10–15 minutes until the cauliflower is tender and golden. Let cool for 10 minutes.

★ Meanwhile, make the blue cheese dressing. Place the sour cream, blue cheese, vinegar and a little salt and pepper in a blender and whizz until fairly smooth. Stir in the chives and sugar; adjust seasoning to taste.

★ To serve, cut the buns in half and toast the cut sides under the grill/broiler. Fill with the lettuce, top with the cauliflower and drizzle over the blue cheese dressing. Serve at once.

OPEN TEX-MEX BURGER
with chilli/chile relish

- -

750 g/1½ lb. beef chuck steak, minced/ground

1 small red onion, finely chopped

1 garlic clove, crushed

2 teaspoons dried oregano

1½ teaspoons ground cumin

sea salt and freshly ground black pepper

olive oil, for brushing

chilli/chile relish

500 g/1 lb. 2 oz. tomatoes, coarsely chopped

1 red onion, coarsely chopped

2 garlic cloves, crushed

2–4 jalapeño chillies/chiles, coarsely chopped

2 tablespoons Worcestershire sauce

200 g/1 cup soft brown sugar

150 ml/⅔ cup red wine vinegar

2 teaspoons sea salt

to serve

2 burger buns, halved

100 g/1 cup shredded iceberg lettuce

100 g/¼ cup grated Cheddar cheese

serves 4

THE FLAVOURS OF TEXAS AND MEXICO COMBINE WELL IN THIS TANGY BURGER. AND FOR THOSE WHO REALLY LIKE IT HOT, TRY THE CARIBBEAN VERSION WITH THE FIERY CHILLI/CHILE SAUCE.

★ To make the chilli/chile relish, put the tomatoes, onion, garlic and chillies/chiles in a food processor and blend until smooth. Transfer the mixture to a saucepan, add the Worcestershire sauce, sugar, vinegar and sea salt. Bring to the boil and simmer gently for 30–40 minutes until the sauce has thickened. Let cool completely and refrigerate until required.

★ Put the beef, onion, garlic, oregano, cumin and some salt and pepper in a bowl and work together with your hands until slightly sticky and evenly mixed. Divide into four portions and shape into burger patties. Press each burger down to make them nice and flat. Cover and chill for 30 minutes.

★ Brush the patties lightly with olive oil and barbecue or grill/broil for 4–5 minutes on each side until cooked through. Keep them warm.

★ Lightly toast the buns under the grill/broiler. Top each half with shredded lettuce, a patty, some grated cheese and chilli/chile relish. Serve at once.

Variation: Caribbean Chilli/Chile Burger: Make the relish as above, replacing the jalapeño chillies/chiles with 1 Scotch bonnet or habanero chilli/chile, deseeded and chopped. When assembling the burger, add a layer of sliced avocado to help to temper the fire of the extra-hot sauce (use disposable latex gloves when handling Scotch bonnet or habanero chillies/chiles).

CHILLI CON CARNE BURGER
wrapped in grilled courgette/zucchini slices

1 tablespoon olive oil

1 large courgette/zucchini, sliced lengthways into thin slices

200 g/7 oz. lean minced/ground beef

2 tablespoons chopped cooked kidney beans

4 teaspoons tomato purée/paste

½ red onion, finely chopped

3 tablespoons fresh breadcrumbs

1 tablespoon beaten egg

1 fresh red chilli/chile, finely chopped

a pinch of ground cumin

sea salt and freshly ground black pepper

to serve

4 slices of Cheddar cheese

2 wholemeal/wholewheat bread rolls (optional)

2 tablespoons sour cream

Classic Homecut Fries (see page 125)

serves 2

THIS HEARTY RECIPE IS THE BURGER INTERPRETATION OF A TRADITIONAL CHILLI CON CARNE. THESE DELICIOUSLY SPICY BURGERS ARE JUST AS GOOD SERVED ON OPEN BREAD ROLLS OR EATEN SIMPLY AS THEY ARE.

★ Preheat the grill/broiler to medium.

★ Heat the oil in a ridged stovetop grill pan. Add the courgette/zucchini slices and cook over a high heat, turning occasionally, until browned on each side. Set aside to cool.

★ Put the beef in a bowl with the kidney beans, tomato purée/paste, onion, breadcrumbs, egg, chilli/chile, cumin and salt and pepper. Work together with your hands until evenly mixed. Divide the beef mixture in half and shape into two burger patties. Squeeze them together to keep the ingredients well packed inside, then press each burger down to make them nice and flat.

★ Put the burgers on a baking sheet and grill/broil for 5 minutes on each side until cooked through. When the burgers are cooked, remove from the grill/broiler and top each with two cheese slices. Wrap a slice of cooled courgette/zucchini around each burger and then fold the slices of courgette/zucchini over the top so they meet in the middle.

★ Slice the bread rolls in half, if using, and put a wrapped burger on the bottom half of each bread roll. Serve at once with with sour cream for spooning and Classic Homecut Fries on the side.

Ingredients

500 g/1 lb. 2 oz. fresh tuna steaks

grated zest and juice of 2 limes

2 spring onions/scallions, trimmed and chopped

1 garlic clove, crushed

50 g/1 cup soft white breadcrumbs

salt and freshly ground black pepper

olive oil, for frying

jerk spice mix

1 tablespoon allspice berries

1 teaspoon chilli flakes/hot red pepper flakes

2 tablespoons soft brown sugar

½ teaspoon ground cinnamon

¼ teaspoon ground cumin

¼ teaspoon ground cloves

to serve

100 g/½ cup Classic Mayo (see page 128)

1 teaspoon Tabasco sauce

1 avocado

1 jalapeno chilli/chile, sliced

a handful of coriander/cilantro leaves

4 sesame bagels or buns

4 lettuce leaves

serves 2

JAMAICAN JERK TUNA BURGER with Tabasco mayonnaise

A TRIPLE WHAMMY OF HEAT IN THIS BURGER WITH THE JERK SPICE IN THE TUNA, THE AVOCADO SALSA AND THE TABASCO IN THE MAYONNAISE – IF ISN'T HOT, IT ISN'T JAMAICAN.

★ Make the jerk spice mix. Place the allspice berries in a small frying pan/skillet and heat gently over a medium heat for 1–2 minutes until they start to release their aroma. Allow to cool, then grind with the chilli/red pepper flakes using a pestle and mortar or spice grinder. Combine with the sugar and ground spices. (Any spice mix not used in this recipe can be stored in a jar.)

★ Make the burgers. Dice the tuna and place in a food processor with 1 tablespoon of the jerk spice mix, the grated zest and juice of 1 lime, spring onions/scallions, garlic, breadcrumbs and a little salt and pepper. Using the pulse button, gradually blend the mixture until chopped but not mushy. Divide the mixture in half and shape into two burger patties. Press each burger down to make them nice and flat. Chill for 30 minutes.

★ Combine the Classic Mayo and Tabasco in a bowl.

★ Peel and stone the avocado and thickly slice. Combine with the chilli/chile, coriander/cilantro leaves and the zest and juice of the remaining lime and season to taste.

★ Preheat a ridged stovetop grill pan over a high heat. Brush the patties with a little oil and cook for 3 minutes on each side until charred. Rest for 5 minutes.

★ To serve, cut the bagels in half and toast the cut sides under the grill/broiler. Assemble the bagels with the lettuce leaves, tuna burgers, avocado salsa and Tabasco mayonnaise. Serve at once.

1 sweet potato, peeled and chopped into 2.5-cm/1-in. cubes

3 garlic cloves, skins on

olive oil, for drizzling

40 g/3 tablespoons Puy lentils (or other green lentils)

1 teaspoon vegetable bouillon powder

60 g/½ cup fresh wholemeal/whole-wheat breadcrumbs

1 carrot, grated

6–8 sun-dried tomatoes, finely chopped

1 medium–hot red chilli/chile, deseeded and finely chopped

1 teaspoon balsamic vinegar

1 teaspoon dried oregano

1 teaspoon dark soy sauce

1 teaspoon Cajun spice blend

1 small egg, lightly beaten

1 tablespoon plain/all-purpose flour

1 tablespoon polenta/cornmeal

celery salt and freshly ground black pepper

to serve

8 burger buns, warmed

rocket/arugula leaves

red onion relish

serves 8

CHILLI VEGGIE BURGER
with sun-dried tomatoes

THESE SWEET POTATO AND LENTIL BURGERS ARE DELICIOUSLY SAVOURY AND JUST SPICY ENOUGH, WITH SWEET HINTS FROM THE SUN-DRIED TOMATOES. THE POLENTA/CORNMEAL COATING GIVES THEM A PLEASING HINT OF CRUNCH TOO.

★ Preheat the oven to 160°C (325°F) Gas 3.

★ Put the sweet potato in a roasting dish with the garlic and drizzle liberally with olive oil. Roast in the preheated oven for about 40 minutes, or until the potato is soft and just beginning to colour around the edges. Remove from the oven and let cool slightly.

★ Meanwhile, place the lentils in a pan of cold water with the vegetable bouillon, bring to the boil, then reduce the heat to a simmer and cook for 20–25 minutes until tender. Once the lentils are ready, drain them and place in a large mixing bowl. To the lentils, add the breadcrumbs, carrot, sun-dried tomatoes, chilli/chile, vinegar, oregano, soy sauce and Cajun spice blend.

★ Add the cooled sweet potato. Make sure the garlic is cool too, then squeeze it out from its skin into the mix too. Work together with your hands until evenly mixed. Season with celery salt and pepper. Add the egg to the mix to bind everything together – again, it is easiest to use your hands to do this. If the burger mix is too wet, add another handful of breadcrumbs to it.

★ Mix the flour and polenta/cornmeal together in a wide dish or shallow bowl. Form the burger mix into eight equal balls, roll in the flour and polenta mix. Press each burger down to make them nice and flat. Cover with clingfilm/plastic wrap until ready to cook.

★ Heat a little olive oil in a frying pan/skillet and fry the burgers over a medium heat for about 5 minutes each side, turning frequently. Serve at once in warm buns with rocket/arugula leaves and red onion relish.

700 g/1½ lb. skinless boneless chicken breasts, coarsely chopped

50 g/1 cup fresh white breadcrumbs

freshly grated zest of 1 unwaxed lime

2 teaspoons Creole seasoning

2–3 tablespoons plain/all-purpose flour, seasoned with salt and pepper

2 eggs, lightly beaten

100 g/¾ cup medium polenta/cornmeal

sea salt and freshly ground black pepper

sunflower oil, for shallow frying

Creole salsa

2 tomatoes, chopped

½ red onion, finely chopped

1 jalapeño chilli/chile, finely chopped

freshly squeezed juice of 1 lime

1 tablespoon chopped fresh coriander/cilantro

to serve

4 burger buns, halved

100 g/1 cup shredded cos/romaine lettuce

4 tablespoons Classic Mayo (see page 128)

Hot & Smoky Barbecue Sauce (see page 126), to serve

serves 4

CREOLE SPICED CHICKEN BURGER

CREOLE COOKING IS MAINLY ASSOCIATED WITH THE SOUTHERN UNITED STATES AND THE MISSISSIPPI DELTA, WHERE TRADITIONS OF FRENCH, SPANISH AND AFRICAN FOODS COMBINE. READY-MADE SPICE MIXES ARE AVAILABLE FROM SUPERMARKETS AND SPECIALIST FOOD SHOPS.

★ Put the chicken and a tablespoon of water in a food processor and pulse until just minced. Add the breadcrumbs, lime zest, Creole seasoning and some salt and pepper and pulse until smooth. Transfer the mixture to a bowl, cover and chill for 30 minutes.

★ Divide the mixture into eight portions and shape into burger patties. Press each burger down to make them nice and flat. Dust the patties lightly with seasoned flour, then dip them first into the egg and then the polenta/cornmeal to coat thoroughly.

★ Heat a shallow layer of oil in a non-stick frying pan/skillet and when hot, add the patties and fry for 3 minutes on each side until golden and cooked through. Drain on paper towels and keep them warm.

★ Meanwhile, to make the salsa, put the tomatoes, onion, chilli/chile, lime juice and coriander/cilantro in a bowl and season to taste with salt and pepper. Mix well and set aside until required.

★ Lightly toast the buns under the grill/broiler, top one half with lettuce, 2 patties, some Classic Mayo, the salsa and some Hot & Smoky Barbecue Sauce. Add the top of the bun and serve at once.

750 g/1½ lb. premium minced/ground pork

2 garlic cloves, crushed

1 teaspoon grated fresh ginger

2 tablespoons chopped fresh coriander/cilantro

2 tablespoons cornflour/cornstarch

1 egg, lightly beaten

sea salt and freshly ground black pepper

sunflower oil, for brushing

satay sauce

4 tablespoons crunchy peanut butter

2 tablespoons coconut cream

2 tablespoons freshly squeezed lime juice

1 tablespoon sweet chilli/chile sauce, plus extra for serving

2 teaspoons light soy sauce

1 teaspoon soft brown sugar

to serve

4 oval/hero rolls

a handful of fresh herbs, such as Thai or plain basil, coriander/cilantro and mint leaves

12 bamboo skewers, soaked in cold water for 30 minutes

serves 4

SPICED PORK BURGER
with satay sauce

- -

THIS BURGER IS INSPIRED BY SOME OF THE WONDERFUL PORK SKEWERS SERVED IN THAI RESTAURANTS, WITH THEIR GREAT USE OF FRESH HERBS AND SATAY SAUCE.

★ Put the pork, garlic, ginger, coriander/cilantro, cornflour/cornstarch, egg and salt and pepper to taste in a bowl and work together with your hands until evenly mixed. Divide into 12 portions and shape into small logs. Cover and chill for 30 minutes.

★ Meanwhile, to make the satay sauce, put the peanut butter, coconut cream, lime juice, chilli/chile sauce, soy sauce and brown sugar in a small saucepan and heat gently, stirring until mixed. Simmer gently for 1–2 minutes until thickened. Set aside to cool.

★ Thread the patties onto the soaked skewers and brush with oil. Barbecue or grill/broil for 6–8 minutes, turning frequently, until charred on the outside and cooked through. Keep them warm.

★ To serve, split the rolls down the middle, open out and fill with herbs, reserving some for garnish if wished. Remove the skewers from the pork patties and add the patties to the rolls along with some satay sauce and sweet chilli/chile sauce. Serve at once.

SPICY VEGAN BURGERS
with sweet potato wedges

- -

80 g/¾ cup grated vegetables
(root vegetables work well)

50 g/⅓ cup finely diced onion

3 garlic cloves, crushed

1 teaspoon barbecue spice mix

¼ teaspoon sweet paprika

¼ teaspoon ground turmeric

⅛ teaspoon chilli/chili powder

4 tablespoons finely chopped
herbs (parsley, chives, etc.)

575 g/3⅓ cups cooked brown
rice, at room temperature

¾ teaspoon sea salt

plain/all-purpose flour, for
coating

sunflower oil, for frying

pickles and red onion slices,
to serve

Sweet Potato Wedges
(see page 124), to serve

serves 4–5

MAKING A GOOD VEGAN BURGER IS A TRICKY BUSINESS, BUT THIS
RECIPE, WITH ITS FINE CRUST AND JUICY INSIDES, IS THE ANSWER!
THEY DON'T FALL APART OR SOAK UP TOO MUCH OIL. AND THE BAKED
SWEET POTATO WEDGES ARE A HEALTHIER ALTERNATIVE TO FRIES.

★ For the burgers, put all the ingredients (except the flour and the oil) in a big bowl. Work together with your hands until evenly mixed, kneading the rice into the mixture until it starts becoming sticky. This will prevent the burgers from falling apart or absorbing too much oil. Taste and add more salt and spice if needed – the burgers are usually the spicier part of a meal, so you don't want them bland. Allow the mixture to rest for 30 minutes.

★ With moist hands, shape the mixture into small, neat burgers – aim to make about 14. Roll each one in a little flour and set aside.

★ Meanwhile, fill a deep, heavy-based frying pan/skillet with vegetable oil to a depth of 3 cm/1¼ in. and heat it until the oil starts moving. To test the temperature, throw a small piece of the mixture into the pan: if it immediately starts boiling, it's ready to go. Deep-fry a few burgers at a time, depending on the size of your pan – it should not be overcrowded. When they turn golden brown, remove them from the oil with a slotted spoon and place them on paper towels. They should be golden with a thin crust and a juicy inside, and should only grease your fingers lightly.

★ Serve the burgers at once with the pickles and onion slices and Sweet Potato Wedges.

JAPANESE SALMON KATSU SLIDERS

SMALL SALMON PATTIES COATED IN BREADCRUMBS AND SERVED WITH A KATSU SAUCE MAKE REALLY TASTY FISH SLIDERS. ADD SOME WASABI FOR OPTIONAL HEAT!

1 teaspoon sunflower oil, plus 1 tablespoon for frying

1 teaspoon sesame oil

2 shallots, finely chopped

1 teaspoon grated root ginger

400 g/14 oz. skinless salmon fillets

2 teaspoons miso paste

50 g/1 cup panko breadcrumbs

salt and freshly ground black pepper

katsu sauce

4 tablespoons tomato ketchup

2 tablespoons Worcestershire sauce

2 tablespoons oyster sauce

4 teaspoons caster/granulated sugar

to serve

8 mixed mini rolls

a handful of salad leaves

3 tablespoons pickled ginger

a little wasabi paste (optional)

serves 4

★ Heat 1 teaspoon sunflower oil and the sesame oil in a frying pan/skillet and gently fry the shallots and ginger for 5 minutes until soft. Let cool.

★ Combine 300 g/10½ oz. of the salmon with the shallot mixture, miso paste and a little salt and pepper and purée in a food processor until fairly smooth. Finely dice the remaining salmon and stir through the minced mixture. Shape the mixture into eight small patties, pressing each one down to make them nice and flat, and chill for 30 minutes.

★ Preheat the oven to 190°C (375°F) Gas 5 and line a baking sheet with baking parchment.

★ Meanwhile, make the katsu sauce. Combine all the ingredients in a bowl, stirring to dissolve the sugar. Set aside.

★ Place the panko breadcrumbs in a shallow bowl and dip in the patties, pressing the crumbs over the surface to coat them completely.

★ Heat 1 tablespoon sunflower oil in a large frying pan/skillet and cook the patties for 1 minute on each side over a medium heat. Transfer to the prepared sheet and bake in the preheated oven for 3 minutes until cooked through. Remove from the oven and rest for 5 minutes.

★ To serve, cut the rolls in half and lightly toast the cut sides under the grill/broiler. Fill each roll with a burger, salad leaves, pickled ginger, wasabi (if using) and katsu sauce. Serve at once.

THAI CHICKEN BURGER
with mango & crispy shallots

1 tablespoon peanut or vegetable oil, plus extra for cooking

1 shallot, thinly sliced

1 garlic clove, sliced

2.5-cm/1-in. piece root ginger, peeled and shredded

1½ teaspoons shrimp paste (from Thai and Asian food stores)

1 tablespoon desiccated/shredded coconut

1 teaspoon caster/granulated sugar

500 g/1 lb. 2 oz. skinless chicken thigh fillets, roughly chopped

sweet chilli/chile dressing

1 chilli/chile, sliced

juice of 2 limes

1½ tablespoons Thai fish sauce

2 tablespoons caster/granulated sugar

to serve

4 hot dog rolls

a handful of Asian salad leaves

a handful of fresh herbs (e.g. Thai basil, coriander/cilantro, mint)

1 mango, peeled, stoned and sliced

2 tablespoons crispy fried shallots

serves 4

A LOVELY HOMEMADE SWEET CHILLI/CHILE DRESSING ADDS THAT CLASSIC THAI HOT, SWEET, SALTY AND SOUR FLAVOUR WE LOVE AND IS A PERFECT FOIL TO THE CHICKEN AND MANGO. YOU COULD USE BOUGHT SWEET CHILLI SAUCE, BUT THIS HOMEMADE VERSION IS SO MUCH NICER.

★ Heat the oil in a wok and gently fry the shallot, garlic and ginger for 5 minutes until softened. Stir in the shrimp paste, coconut and sugar and stir-fry for 1 minute until fragrant, then continue to stir until you have a slightly sticky paste mix. Let cool.

★ Place the chicken pieces in a food processor with the cooled spice paste and blend until coarsely minced. Shape into eight small burger patties, Press each burger down to make them nice and flat, then cover and chill for 30 minutes.

★ Meanwhile, make the chilli/chile dressing. Place the ingredients in a bowl and whisk until the sugar is dissolved.

★ Heat a ridged stovetop grill pan over a high heat. Brush the patties with a little oil and cook for 3-4 minutes on each side until charred and cooked through. Rest for 5 minutes.

★ To serve, cut the rolls almost in half and open out wide. Fill with lettuce leaves and herbs. Top each roll with two burgers and mango slices. Drizzle over the dressing and scatter over the crispy shallots. Serve at once.

VIETNAMESE SESAME TOFU BANH MI BURGER with pickled vegetables

HERE TOFU IS MARINATED IN A CHAR SUI SAUCE, THEN GRILLED/BROILED AND SERVED WITH PICKLED VEGETABLES, CHILLIES/CHILES, SALAD LEAVES AND FRESH HERBS, MAKING THIS A DELICIOUS VEGGIE ALTERNATIVE TO THE CLASSIC VIETNAMESE BARBECUE PORK ROLLS, OR BANH MI.

300 g/10½ oz. firm tofu

5 tablespoons hoisin sauce

4 tablespoons honey

4 tablespoons dark soy sauce

2 tablespoons Shaoxing wine

1 teaspoon sesame oil

1 teaspoon Chinese 5-spice powder

pickled vegetables

1 small carrot

½ cucumber

½ small red onion

3½ tablespoons rice wine vinegar

50 g/¼ cup caster/granulated sugar

1 teaspoon salt

to serve

1 French baguette

a handful of salad leaves

a few fresh coriander/cilantro, mint and basil leaves

4 tablespoons Classic Mayo (see page 128)

4 tablespoons sweet chilli/chile sauce

1 tablespoon each black and white sesame seeds

serves 4

★ Make the pickled vegetables. Thinly slice the carrot lengthways, then cut into long thin strips. Deseed and cut the cucumber into long thin strips. Thinly slice the onion. Combine the vegetables in a bowl. Place the vinegar, sugar, 2 tablespoons water and salt in a saucepan and heat gently until the sugar has dissolved. Bring to the boil, then pour over the vegetables. Stir well and set aside to cool.

★ Cut the tofu into eight thick slices and place in a bowl. Combine the hoisin sauce, honey, soy sauce, Shaoxing wine, sesame oil and Chinese 5-spice powder. Pour over the tofu, turning to coat the slices thoroughly and leave to marinate for 30 minutes.

★ Heat a heavy-based frying pan/skillet over a high heat and fry the marinated tofu slices in batches for 2 minutes each side until charred.

★ To serve, cut the baguette into 10-cm/4-in. lengths, then slice each one almost in half horizontally. Fill each one with the salad leaves, fresh herbs, fried tofu and pickled vegetables and drizzle over the Classic Mayo and sweet chilli/chile sauce. Scatter over the sesame seeds and serve at once.

180 g/6 oz. lean minced/ground beef

3 tablespoons breadcrumbs

½ red onion, finely chopped

2 teaspoons tomato purée/paste

20 g/3 tablespoons grated Monterey Jack or sharp Cheddar cheese

freshly grated zest of ½ a lime

½ a fresh red chilli/chile, chopped

1 tablespoon beaten egg

1 tablespoon olive or vegetable oil

sea salt and freshly ground black pepper

guacamole

1 large ripe avocado, peeled and pitted

½ fresh red chilli/chile, finely chopped

1 teaspoon lime juice

a handful of fresh coriander/cilantro

tomato salsa

500 g/1 lb. 2 oz. ripe tomatoes, peeled and diced

½ a red onion, finely chopped

1–2 small green chillies/chiles, deseeded and finely chopped

3 tablespoons lime juice

a pinch of sugar

2 tablespoons finely chopped fresh coriander/cilantro

to serve

2 large flour tortillas

sour cream

a handful of coriander/cilantro, chopped

serves 2

MEXICAN BURGER with sour cream, salsa & guacamole

A FULL-ON MEXICAN FEAST, THIS BURGER CONTAINS ALL THE FEISTY FLAVOURS OF MEXICO AS WELL AS THE ACCOMPANIMENTS, SO THEY POWER THROUGH WITH EVERY BITE. IF YOU LIKE IT HOT, JUST ADD SOME EXTRA CHILLI/CHILE.

★ To make the guacamole, put the avocado in a bowl with the chilli/chile, lime juice, coriander/cilantro and a pinch of sea salt and pepper, to taste. Mash together with a fork.

★ To make the tomato salsa, put the tomatoes in a bowl with the onion and chillies/chiles. Add the lime juice and mix well, then add the sugar and season with sea salt. Stir in the coriander/cilantro.

★ To make the burgers, put the beef in a bowl with the breadcrumbs, onion, tomato purée/paste, cheese, lime zest, chilli/chile, egg and a pinch of sea salt and pepper. Work together with your hands until evenly mixed. Divide the beef mixture in half and shape into two burger patties. Press each burger down to make them nice and flat.

★ Heat the oil in a frying pan/skillet and fry the burgers over a medium–high heat for 5 minutes on each side until cooked through.

★ Preheat the grill/broiler to medium. Splash a few drops of water on each tortilla and lay them under the grill/broiler for a few seconds on each side to lightly toast. Spread both tortillas with sour cream and put a cooked burger on top of each. Top with a spoonful each of guacamole and tomato salsa. Sprinkle with coriander/cilantro and serve, folding the sides of the tortilla around the burger to eat. Serve at once.

SPANISH CHORIZO & BEAN BURGER

400 g/14 oz. lean minced/ground beef

125 g/4½ oz. chorizo, finely diced

80 g/3¼ oz. canned red kidney beans (drained weight), rinsed, drained and crushed

60 g/1 cup breadcrumbs

4 teaspoons tomato purée/paste

1 teaspoon freshly chopped parsley

sea salt and freshly ground black pepper

to serve

4 crusty bread rolls, halved

a handful of salad leaves

Caramelized Red Onions (see page 133)

serves 4

PORK AND BEEF ALWAYS MAKE A GREAT FLAVOUR COMBINATION IN A BURGER AND THIS RECIPE IS NO EXCEPTION, WITH THE ADDITION OF FINELY DICED CHORIZO ADDING AN UNUSUAL TASTE TWIST. THE MIXTURE OF FRESH MINCED/GROUND BEEF WITH A CURED PORK, SUCH AS CHORIZO, WORKS VERY WELL.

★ Put all the burger ingredients in a large bowl and work together with your hands until evenly mixed. Divide the mixture into four and shape into burger patties. Press each burger down to make them nice and flat.

★ To cook the burgers, fry them in a frying pan/skillet over medium heat for 12–15 minutes, turning a few times, until cooked through. Alternatively, pop them under a preheated hot grill/broiler and cook for 6 minutes on each side, until cooked through.

★ Slice the bread rolls in half and light toast the cut sides under the grill/broiler. Add a layer of salad leaves, then top with the hot burgers and a large spoonful of the Caramelized Red Onions. Serve at once.

INDIAN-STYLE LAMB SLIDERS
with minted yogurt & mango chutney

- -

THESE DELICIOUSLY SPICED INDIAN-STYLE SLIDERS PACK A GOOD PUNCH. SERVED ON MINI NAAN BREADS, THEY LOOK GREAT AND MAKE PERFECT CANAPÉS FOR A PARTY OR APPETIZERS FOR AN INDIAN-THEMED FEAST.

200 g/7 oz. lean minced/ground lamb

1 tablespoon garam masala

a pinch of ground turmeric

3 tablespoons fresh breadcrumbs

1 tablespoon beaten egg

a pinch of chopped fresh coriander/cilantro

a pinch of sea salt and freshly ground black pepper

olive oil, for frying

to serve

4 mini naan breads

plain yogurt mixed with freshly chopped mint leaves

mango chutney

cocktail sticks/toothpicks (optional)

serves 4

★ Put the lamb in a bowl with the garam masala, turmeric, breadcrumbs, egg, coriander/cilantro and salt and pepper. Divide the mixture into quarters and shape into four slider patties. Press each slider down to make them nice and flat.

★ Heat the oil in a frying pan/skillet and fry the sliders over medium–high heat for 4 minutes on each side until cooked through.

★ Splash a little water on each of the mini naan breads and toast under the grill/broiler or in a toaster to warm. Put a generous spoonful of minted yogurt over the top of each mini naan. Top with a cooked slider and finish with a spoonful of mango chutney. Put a cocktail stick/toothpick through the middle of each, if needed, and serve at once.

CHINESE CRISPY DUCK SLIDERS
with hoisin & spring onions/scallions

- -

WHAT COULD BE MORE DELICIOUS THAN PEKING DUCK BURGERS? THESE ARE LOVELY ESPECIALLY WITH THE BRIOCHE ROLLS AS AN ALTERNATIVE TO CHINESE STEAMED BUNS; YOU COULD ALSO SUBSTITUTE WITH BAO BUNS IF YOU WANT.

2 x 450 g/1 lb. duck leg confit, at room temperature

2 tablespoons honey

2 tablespoons soy sauce

2 teaspoons hoisin sauce, plus extra to serve

1 teaspoon Chinese 5-spice powder

50 g/6 tablespoons plain/all-purpose flour

2 eggs, beaten

75 g/1 cup dried breadcrumbs

sunflower oil, for frying

to serve

4 spring onions/scallions, trimmed and cut into strips

1 small cucumber, deseeded and cut into thin batons

8 oval or round brioche rolls

a roasting pan, lined with baking parchment

makes 8

★ Preheat the oven to 190°C (375°F) Gas 5.

★ Set 1 tablespoon of fat from the duck confit aside and reserve for later. Discard the remaining fat. Place the duck legs in the prepared roasting pan.

★ Combine the honey, soy sauce and hoisin sauce in a bowl and add a pinch of salt. Brush all over the duck legs and roast in the preheated oven for 15 minutes, brushing with the glaze in the pan halfway through until golden. Let cool.

★ Roughly tear the duck skin and flesh into small pieces and place in a food processor with the reserved fat and the Chinese 5-spice powder and a little salt and pepper. Pulse briefly until the mixture just comes together.

★ Divide the duck mixture into eight small slider patties and press each slider down to make them nice and flat. Dip each one into the flour, then the beaten egg and finally the breadcrumbs, turning over until evenly coated with crumbs. Chill for 30 minutes.

★ Heat about 1 tablespoon sunflower oil in a large frying pan/skillet and fry the patties in batches for 2 minutes on each side until golden. Transfer to a clean baking sheet and bake for a further 5 minutes until cooked through.

★ To serve, cut the brioche rolls in half and lightly toast the cut sides, under the grill/broiler. Fill with the duck sliders, spring onions/scallion strips, cucumber batons and some extra hoisin sauce. Serve at once.

MALAYSIAN PRAWN/SHRIMP SAMBAL SLIDERS

MALAYSIAN SAMBALS, OR SAUCES, ARE A BLEND OF ASIAN AND INDIAN FLAVOURS, AND IT IS THE TURMERIC THAT GIVES THIS ONE ITS DISTINCTIVE COLOUR AND TASTE. IT'S A DELICIOUS COMPLEMENT TO THE CHARRED PRAWNS/SHRIMP.

16 large raw prawns/shrimp, peeled and deveined

1 tablespoon sunflower oil

zest and juice of 1 lime

2 teaspoons caster/granulated sugar

2 teaspoons sea salt

sambal

2 large shallots, chopped

2 Thai red chillies/chiles, seeded and chopped

2 large garlic cloves, sliced

½ teaspoon ground turmeric

1 tablespoons peanut oil

2 tablespoons coconut cream

1 tablespoon tamarind paste

1 tablespoon light soy sauce

2 tablespoons white sugar

1 large tomato, diced

salt and freshly ground black pepper

to serve

8 mini brioche rolls

a handful of Asian salad leaves

4 tablespoons Classic Mayo (see page 128)

a few coriander/cilantro leaves

16 bamboo skewers, soaked

serves 4

★ Make the sambal. Place the shallots, chillies/chiles, garlic, turmeric and a pinch of salt in a food processor with 1 tablespoon water and blend until smooth. Heat the peanut oil in a small wok or frying pan/skillet and gently fry the paste for 5 minutes over a very low heat until fragrant. Stir in the coconut cream, tamarind paste, soy sauce and sugar and cook, stirring, for 1 minute, then add the tomato. Simmer gently for 10 minutes until the sauce has thickened. Leave to cool.

★ Place the prawns/shrimp in a shallow dish and combine with the sunflower oil, lime zest, sugar and salt. Thread the prawns/shrimp lengthways onto the soaked bamboo skewers to keep them as flat as you can and marinate for 15 minutes.

★ Heat a ridged stovetop griddle pan over a high heat and cook the prawns/shrimp for 1–2 minutes on each side until charred and cooked through. Remove from the heat and dress with the lime juice. Rest for 3 minutes.

★ To serve, cut the rolls in half and lightly toast the cut sides under a grill/broiler. Fill with salad leaves, sambal, prawns/shrimp, Classic Mayo and coriander/cilantro. Serve at once.

MEDITERRANEAN LAMB BURGER

750 g/1½ lb. premium minced/ground lamb

1 small onion, finely chopped

1 tablespoon chopped fresh mint leaves

2 teaspoons dried oregano

6 anchovies in oil, drained and chopped

sea salt and freshly ground black pepper

to serve

4 plum tomatoes, halved

4 slices ciabatta or focaccia

1 garlic clove, left whole

150 g/6 oz. mozzarella cheese, sliced

a handful of fresh basil leaves

olive oil, for brushing and drizzling

Rocket/Arugula, Radicchio and Crispy Bacon Salad (see page 136)

serves 4

LAMB MAKES A LOVELY ALTERNATIVE TO BEEF. YOU COULD USE DICED LEG OR SHOULDER, AND MINCE OR PROCESS IT COARSELY YOURSELF. THIS BURGER GOES SUPERBLY WITH A ROCKET/ARUGULA, RADICCHIO AND CRISPY BACON SALAD.

★ Put the lamb, onion, mint, oregano, anchovies and some salt and pepper in a bowl and work together with your hands until evenly mixed. Divide into four portions and shape into burger patties. Press each burger down to make them nice and flat. Cover and chill for 30 minutes.

★ Brush the patties lightly with olive oil and barbecue or grill/broil for 4–5 minutes on each side until cooked through. Keep them warm.

★ Meanwhile, arrange the tomato halves on a ridged stovetop grill pan, season with salt and pepper and drizzle with a little olive oil. Cook under a preheated hot grill/broiler for 2–3 minutes until softened.

★ Barbecue or grill/broil the ciabatta or focaccia slices and rub all over with the whole garlic and drizzle with oil. Transfer to serving plates and top each with a patty, mozzarella, a grilled tomato and some basil. Serve at once with the Rocket/Arugula, Radicchio and Bacon Salad.

ITALIAN BURGER
with olives, sun-dried tomatoes & pesto

- -

HERE A FEW SIMPLE INGREDIENTS PRODUCE THIS HEARTY AND HEAVENLY BURGER WITH ALL THE CLASSIC FLAVOURS OF ITALY. SERVE IN A CIABATTA ROLL TO CONTINUE THE ITALIAN THEME.

220 g/8 oz. lean minced/ground beef

4 pitted black olives, finely chopped

2 sun-dried tomatoes, finely chopped

2 teaspoons tomato purée/paste

2 teaspoons pesto

a pinch of sea salt and freshly ground black pepper

to serve

2 ciabatta rolls

Pesto Mayo (see page 129)

a bowl of black olives (optional)

serves 2

★ Preheat the grill/broiler to medium.

★ Put the beef in a bowl with the olives, sun-dried tomatoes, tomato purée/paste, pesto and salt and pepper. Work together with your hands until evenly mixed. Divide the beef mixture in half and shape into two burger patties. Press each burger down to make them nice and flat.

★ Put the burgers on a baking sheet and grill/broil for 5 minutes on each side until cooked through. Remove from the grill/broiler and set aside. Leave the grill/broiler on.

★ Slice the ciabatta rolls in half and lightly toast them under the hot grill/broiler.

★ Put a burger on the bottom half of each ciabatta roll and top with a large spoonful of Pesto Mayo. Finish the burgers with the lids of the ciabatta rolls and serve with a bowl of olives on the side, if liked.

CHRISTMAS CANAPÉ SLIDERS
with cranberry sauce & Camembert

- -

1 parsnip, cut into 1-cm/¾-in. slices

1 tablespoon runny honey

160 g/5½ oz. lean minced/ground turkey

1 tablespoon beaten egg

2 teaspoons tomato purée/paste

3 cooked chestnuts, finely chopped

3 tablespoons fresh breadcrumbs

1 tablespoon olive or vegetable oil

sea salt and freshly ground black pepper

to serve

5 squares of Camembert cheese

cranberry sauce

5 cocktail sticks/toothpicks

makes 5

THESE SEASONAL SLIDERS ARE PERFECT SERVED AS FESTIVE CANAPÉS OR APPETIZERS FOR A WINTER MENU. THEY ARE ALSO GREAT FOR USING UP ANY TURKEY LEFTOVERS YOU MAY HAVE DURING THE HOLIDAY SEASON.

★ Preheat the oven to 180°C (350°F) Gas 4.

★ Put the parsnip in a baking dish, drizzle with the honey and toss to coat. Bake in the preheated oven for 25–30 minutes until soft and starting to brown. Remove from the oven and leave to cool.

★ Put the turkey in a bowl with the egg, tomato purée/paste, chestnuts, breadcrumbs and salt and pepper. Divide the mixture into five equal pieces and shape into five slider patties. Press each slider down to make them nice and flat.

★ Heat the oil in a frying pan/skillet and fry the sliders over a medium–high heat for 4 minutes on each side until cooked through.

★ Put the sliders on a serving plate and cover each with a square of Camembert. Top the sliders with a slice of roasted parsnip and put a cocktail stick/toothpick through the middle of each slider to hold them in place. Serve at once with a bowl of cranberry sauce for spooning.

450–680 g/1–1½ lb. extra lean minced/ground beef

2 spring onions/scallions, diced

1 teaspoon sea salt

1 teaspoon freshly ground black pepper

½ tablespoon olive oil

1 egg

secret sauce

115 g/½ cup Classic Mayo (see page 128)

2 tablespoons creamy French dressing

3 tablespoons chopped Home Pickled Cucumber (see page 132)

½ small white onion, finely diced

1 teaspoon vinegar

1 teaspoon granulated sugar

a pinch of sea salt

to serve

8–12 slices American or Cheddar cheese

8–12 slider buns

iceberg lettuce, cut into strips

gherkins, sliced

Sweet Potato Wedges (see page 124)

makes 8–12

SECRET-SAUCE SLIDERS

POPULARIZED IN NEW YORK IN THE 1990S, THESE TASTY MINI-BURGERS ARE THE QUINTESSENTIAL AMERICAN SNACK AND WILL NEVER FAIL TO BRING A SMILE TO YOUR FACE! THEY'RE JUST THE RIGHT SIZE FOR A QUICK FIX AND GREAT TO SERVE TO A CROWD.

★ In a medium mixing bowl, combine the minced/ground beef, spring onions/scallions, salt, pepper, olive oil and egg. Mix well with your hands and then press the meat mixture into slider patties. You can use a cookie cutter to get even and equal-sized sliders. Press each slider down to make them nice and flat. This recipe makes 8–12 sliders depending on the size you prefer.

★ In a small mixing bowl, combine the secret sauce ingredients and season to taste.

★ Cook the sliders under a grill/broiler or pan-fry them to your liking. Place a slice of cheese on top of the hot slider to let it melt a little.

★ Meanwhile, cut the slider buns in half and spread the sauce on the bottom half. Chop the iceberg lettuce into strips and place a few on top of the sauce. Put the slider and cheese on top, followed by more secret sauce and a couple of sliced gherkins. Add the top half of the bun.

★ Serve the sliders at once with extra sliced gherkins on the side and a bowl of Sweet Potato Wedges.

1 tablespoon canned black beans

1 spring onion/scallion, sliced

1 garlic clove, finely chopped

2 teaspoons tomato purée/paste

a pinch of cayenne pepper

1 tablespoon chopped fresh coriander/cilantro

200 g/7 oz. lean minced/ground beef

40 g/3 tablespoons long grain rice, cooked and cooled

1 tablespoon olive or vegetable oil

a pinch of sea salt and freshly ground black pepper

corn & pepper salsa

2 large corn cobs/ears of corn

3 tablespoons vegetable oil

4 spring onions/scallions, sliced

freshly squeezed juice of 1 lime

6 Pepperdew peppers, diced

2 tablespoons finely chopped coriander/cilantro

a dash of chilli/chile sauce

sea salt and freshly ground black pepper

to serve

4 mini poppyseed rolls

Lime Mayo (see page 129)

Sweet Potato Wedges (see page 124)

makes 4

BEEF & BLACK BEAN SLIDERS with corn & pepper salsa

CAPTURE THE TASTE OF SOUTH AMERICA WHEREVER YOU ARE WITH THESE DELICIOUS BEEF SLIDERS. SERVED WITH SPICY CORN AND PEPPER SALSA AND TANGY LIME MAYO, THESE ARE GUARANTEED TO CREATE A FIESTA OF FLAVOURS FOR YOUR TASTEBUDS.

★ To make the Corn and Pepper Salsa, cut down the sides of the corn cobs with a sharp knife to remove the kernels. Heat 2 teaspoons of the oil in a frying pan/skillet set over medium heat. Add the corn and cook for 2–3 minutes until it begins to brown. Add the spring onions/scallions and cook for 1 minute. Transfer to a bowl and let cool.

★ Add the lime juice, peppers, coriander/cilantro and the remaining oil, and mix well. Add a dash of chilli/chile sauce and season with salt and pepper.

★ To make the sliders, blitz the black beans, spring onion/scallion, garlic, tomato purée/paste, cayenne pepper and and coriander/cilantro in a food processor. Tip the mixture into a mixing bowl, add the beef and work together with your hands until evenly mixed. Add the cooled rice, season with salt and pepper and mix again.

★ Divide the beef mixture into quarters and shape into four slider patties. Press each slider down to make them nice and flat.

★ Heat the oil in a frying pan/skillet and fry the sliders over a medium–high heat for 4 minutes on each side until cooked through.

★ Slice the mini poppyseed rolls in half and spread the bottom half of each with Lime Mayo. Put a cooked slider on top of each and add a large spoonful of Corn and Pepper Salsa. Finish the sliders with the lids of the rolls and serve with Sweet Potato Wedges on the side, if liked.

200 g/7 oz. lean minced/ground chicken or turkey

6 chives, finely chopped

1 teaspoon anchovy paste

20 g/⅓ cup Parmesan cheese, finely grated

1 teaspoon beaten egg

a pinch of sea salt and freshly ground black pepper

2 slices of Parma ham, cut in half

Caesar dressing

1 egg yolk

1 small garlic clove, crushed

2 anchovy fillets in oil, drained and chopped

1 tablespoon freshly squeezed lemon juice

1 teaspoon Worcestershire sauce

150 ml/⅔ cup olive oil

25 g/½ cup Parmesan cheese, finely grated

sea salt and freshly ground black pepper

to serve

4 seeded mini rolls

a handful of Romano lettuce leaves

4 cocktail sticks/toothpicks

makes 4

CHICKEN CAESAR SLIDERS
wrapped in Parma ham

- -

THESE CUTE SLIDERS COMBINE ALL THE INGREDIENTS OF A CHICKEN CAESAR SALAD. THEY'RE LIGHT AND DELICIOUS AND MAKE GREAT CANAPÉS TO SERVE AT PARTIES – PERFECT FOR ENTERTAINING.

★ Preheat the oven to 180°C (350°F) Gas 4.

★ To make the Caesar dressing, whisk the egg yolk in a small bowl with the garlic, anchovies, lemon juice, Worcestershire sauce and salt and pepper, to taste, until frothy. Gradually whisk in the olive oil a little at a time until thick and glossy. Add 2 tablespoons of water to thin the dressing and stir in the Parmesan. Store in a screw-top jar in the fridge and use the same day.

★ To make the sliders, put the chicken in a bowl with the chives, anchovy paste, Parmesan, egg and salt and pepper. Work together with your hands until evenly mixed. Divide the mixture into quarters and shape into four slider patties. Press each slider down to make them nice and flat.

★ Wrap a piece of Parma ham around each slider and lay them on a baking sheet. Bake in the preheated oven for 15–20 minutes until cooked through.

★ Cut each of the rolls in half and put a Romano lettuce leaf on the bottom half of each roll. Top each with a cooked slider, drizzle with Caesar dressing and finish with the lids of the rolls. Put a cocktail stick/toothpick through the middle of each slider to hold it in place and serve at once.

HONEY APPLE PORK SLIDERS
with caramelized apple slices

1 Bramley, or other tart apple, peeled and grated

2 tablespoons clear honey

200 g/7 oz. lean minced/ground pork

1 tablespoon olive or vegetable oil

a pinch of sea salt

caramelized apple slices

1 tablespoon butter

1 Bramley, or other tart apple, sliced

1 tablespoon brown sugar

to serve

4 mini wholemeal/wholewheat bread rolls

a handful of rocket/arugula leaves

Homemade Tomato Ketchup (see page 127)

makes 4

THESE TASTY LITTLE PORK BITES ARE OOZING WITH DELICIOUS CARAMELIZED APPLE SLICES. THEY ARE PERFECT FOR PARTIES, POPULAR WITH CHILDREN AND SO EASY! IF YOU HAVE ANY LITTLE ONES AROUND, YOU CAN EVEN ASK THEM TO HELP YOU MAKE THEM.

★ Preheat the oven to 180°C (350°F) Gas 4.

★ To make the sliders, lay the grated apple on a baking sheet and drizzle the honey over the top. Mix well to coat, then bake in the preheated oven for 20–25 minutes until brown and soft, stirring once or twice during cooking. Remove from the oven and set aside to cool.

★ Put the pork in a bowl with the salt and add the cooled apple. Work together with your hands until evenly mixed. Divide the mixture into quarters and shape into four slider patties. Press each slider down to make them nice and flat. Chill in the fridge while you make the caramelized apple slices.

★ To make the caramelized apple slices, heat the butter in a frying pan/skillet set over medium-high heat until bubbling. Add the apple slices and cook until tender, crisp and beginning to brown, turning the slices in the pan to brown evenly. Add the sugar and cook until melted and starting to caramelize. Remove from the heat and set aside to cool slightly.

★ Heat the oil in a frying pan/skillet and fry the sliders over medium–high heat for 4 minutes on each side until cooked through.

★ Slice the mini bread rolls in half and put a few rocket/arugula leaves on the bottom of each. Add the cooked sliders and top each with a slice of caramelized apple. Finish the sliders with the lids of the rolls and serve at once with Homemade Tomato Ketchup, if liked.

LAMB & MINT SLIDERS
with roast potatoes & watercress

3 tablespoons olive oil

8 roughly-equal rounds of potato, unpeeled

200 g/7 oz. lean minced/ground lamb

6 fresh mint leaves, finely chopped

3 tablespoons fresh breadcrumbs

1 tablespoon beaten egg

a pinch of sea salt and freshly ground black pepper

a handful of watercress, to serve

4 cocktail sticks/toothpicks

makes 4

- -

CREATE A ROAST LAMB DINNER IN MINIATURE FORM WITH THESE GOURMET SLIDERS. THEY TASTE GREAT IN A BUN, BUT EVEN BETTER SERVED INSIDE TWO ROAST POTATO ROUNDS.

★ Preheat the oven to 180°C (350°F) Gas 4.

★ Sprinkle 1 tablespoon of the oil on a baking sheet and place the potato slices on top, mix to coat and sprinkle with black pepper. Bake in the preheated oven for 25 minutes until brown and crisp. Remove from the oven and set aside until cool enough to handle.

★ Put the lamb in a bowl with the mint, breadcrumbs, egg and salt and pepper. Work together with your hands until evenly mixed. Divide the mixture into quarters and shape into four slider patties. Press each slider down to make them nice and flat.

★ Heat the remaining oil in a frying pan/skillet and fry the sliders over a medium–high heat for 4 minutes on each side until cooked through.

★ Put one potato round on each serving plate and put a cooked slider on top of each. Top with a few leaves of watercress and finish with another potato round. Put a cocktail stick/toothpick through the middle of each slider to hold them together and serve at once.

TURKEY BURGER

with onion & cranberry jam/relish

----

625 g/1½ lb. skinless turkey breast fillet, coarsely chopped

125 g/4 slices of smoked streaky/ fatty bacon, coarsely chopped

2 tablespoons wholegrain mustard

2 tablespoons chopped fresh flat-leaf parsley

½ teaspoon smoked paprika

sea salt and freshly ground black pepper

sunflower oil, for shallow frying

onion & cranberry jam/relish

2 tablespoons olive oil

2 red onions, thinly sliced

50 g/⅓ cup dried cranberries

1 tablespoon balsamic vinegar

100 g/½ cup cranberry sauce

to serve

4 burger buns, halved

a handful of watercress

serves 4

HERE TURKEY MINCE IS FLAVOURED WITH WHOLEGRAIN MUSTARD AND THE COOKED BURGER IS SERVED WITH DELICIOUS ONION AND CRANBERRY JAM/RELISH.

★ To make the onion and cranberry jam/relish, heat the oil in a saucepan, add the onions and fry over medium heat for 20–25 minutes until caramelized, stirring occasionally.

★ Meanwhile, soak the cranberries in the vinegar until required. Add to the onions with the cranberry sauce and 2 tablespoons water and cook for 10 minutes until thickened and jam-like. Season to taste with salt and pepper and set aside to cool.

★ Put the turkey and bacon in a food processor and blend until coarsely minced. Transfer to a bowl, add the mustard, parsley, paprika and some salt and pepper and work together with your hands until evenly mixed. Cover and chill for 30 minutes. Divide into four portions and shape into burger patties. Press each burger down to make them nice and flat.

★ Heat a shallow layer of sunflower oil in a frying pan/skillet, add the turkey patties and fry for 4–5 minutes on each side until cooked through. Keep them warm.

★ Lightly toast the buns under the grill/broiler and fill with watercress, patties and the onion and cranberry jam/relish. Serve at once.

'SAUSAGE' BURGER FOR KIDS

KIDS LOVE BURGERS AND THESE ARE SERVED AS SAUSAGE SHAPES IN A HOT DOG ROLL. ALTERNATIVELY, YOU COULD SHAPE THEM AS THE MORE TRADITIONAL PATTIES AND SERVE IN SMALL TOASTED BUNS. YOU CAN ALSO ADD SOME SHREDDED LETTUCE AND TOMATOES TO THE BURGER FOR A HEALTHIER OPTION.

500 g/1 lb. 2 oz. premium minced/ground beef

2 teaspoons onion powder

2 tablespoons Homemade Tomato Ketchup (see page 127), plus extra to serve

2 tablespoons freshly chopped flat-leaf parsley

sea salt and freshly ground black pepper

olive oil, for brushing

to serve

8 hot dog rolls

100 g/¼ cup grated Cheddar cheese

serves 4

★ Put the beef, onion powder, tomato ketchup, parsley and a little salt and pepper in a bowl and work together with your hands until evenly mixed and slightly sticky. Divide into four portions and form into long thin sausage shapes. Cover and chill for 30 minutes.

★ Brush the 'sausage' burgers lightly with olive oil and cook on a preheated ridged stovetop grill pan (or a heavy frying pan/skillet) for 7–8 minutes, turning frequently until cooked through.

★ Split the rolls horizontally without cutting all the way through. Put a 'sausage' into each one and sprinkle with some grated cheese and Homemade Tomato Ketchup.
Serve at once.

MINI PARTY HAMBURGERS

500 g/1 lb. 2 oz. lean beef, finely minced (or half pork and half beef)

4 shallots or small onions, finely chopped

3 garlic cloves, crushed

1 red chilli/chile, deseeded and finely chopped

1 egg, beaten

a pinch of freshly ground nutmeg

4 tablespoons/¼ cup fresh white breadcrumbs

salt and freshly ground black pepper

peanut oil, for frying

to serve

40 mini hamburger buns

Hot & Smoky Barbecue Sauce (see page 126) or chilli/chile sauce

baby salad and herb leaves

10 cherry tomatoes, sliced

4 baby onions, finely sliced

40 baby cornichons/gherkins

cocktail sticks/toothpicks

makes 40

THE QUANTITIES GIVEN HERE WILL MAKE 40 SLIDER-SIZED BURGERS – PERFECT WHEN FEEDING A CROWD. IF YOU WISH, YOU CAN PREPARE THE PATTIES IN ADVANCE AND CHILL IN THE FRIDGE UNTIL YOU ARE READY TO COOK THEM.

★ Put all the patty ingredients except the oil in a bowl and mix well. Take 1 tablespoon of the mixture and shape into a round, flat patty. Repeat until all the mixture is used.

★ Preheat the oven to 200°C (400°F) Gas 6.

★ Heat a film of oil in a heavy-based frying pan/skillet until very hot, then add a layer of patties, spaced well apart. Fry for 2–3 minutes, turning half way, until cooked through. Remove from the pan, drain on crumpled kitchen paper and keep warm while you cook the remaining patties.

★ Heat up the buns in the preheated oven for about 5 minutes, then split, leaving one side attached if possible. Put a dot of Smoky Barbecue Sauce or chilli/chile sauce into each bun, then a salad leaf, a patty, tomato and onion ring. Put the lid on the bun and secure with a cocktail stick/toothpick and a mini cornichon. Serve at once.

SURPRISE BURGER

HERE'S A DIFFERENT TAKE ON THE TRADITIONAL CHEESEBURGER –
A HIDDEN PIECE OF CHEDDAR CHEESE RIGHT IN THE CENTRE!
KIDS WILL ENJOY HELPING TO MAKE THESE BURGERS – LET THEM
SQUELCH THE MIXTURE INTO PATTIES AND MOULD IT AROUND
THE CHEESE.

500 g/1 lb. 2 oz. minced/ground
beef

2 teaspoons tomato sauce

1 tablespoon teriyaki sauce

4 spring onions/scallions, finely
chopped

1 egg, lightly beaten

125 g/4 oz. Cheddar cheese, cut
into 8 small pieces

flour, for dusting

vegetable oil, for brushing

to serve

8 small bread rolls

tomato salsa

8 small cos/romaine lettuce leaves

makes 8

★ Mix together the beef, tomato sauce, teriyaki sauce, spring onions/
scallions and egg in a large bowl. With damp hands, divide the mixture
into eight portions and shape into burger patties.

★ Insert a piece of cheese in the centre of each patty. Wrap the meat
around the cheese and shape into a burger. Press each burger down to
make them nice and flat. Place on a lightly floured plate and chill for
30 minutes.

★ Brush the burgers with oil and cook on a cast-iron griddle pan or
under a hot grill for 5–8 minutes on each side.

★ Split the rolls in half and lightly toast the cut side under the grill/
broiler.

★ Top the bases with the cooked burgers, tomato salsa and a lettuce leaf,
then add the top of the roll. Serve at once.

CHAPTER 5

MEAT-FREE TREATS

COURGETTE/ZUCCHINI SLIDERS
with crispy kale, pesto & whipped feta

2 courgettes/zucchini (about 500 g/1 lb. 2 oz.)

grated zest and juice of 1 lemon

1 tablespoon extra virgin olive oil

salt and freshly ground black pepper

8 small poppy seed rolls

crispy kale

100 g/3½ oz. kale, trimmed

1 tablespoon olive oil

2 teaspoons sesame seeds

rocket/arugula pesto

2 tablespoons pumpkin seeds

60 g/2½ oz. rocket/arugula leaves

1 garlic clove, chopped

3 tablespoons extra virgin olive oil

whipped feta

100 g/3½ oz. feta cheese

2 tablespoons crème fraîche/sour cream

makes 8

LOVELY VIBRANT GREEN SLIDERS SERVED WITH CRISPY KALE LEAVES – PERFECT FOR VEGETARIANS AND MEAT-EATERS ALIKE. YOU WILL NEED THICK CURLY KALE FOR THE CRISPS AS THIS IS MORE ROBUST THAN BABY KALE LEAVES.

★ Trim the courgettes/zucchini and cut lengthways into 3-mm/⅛-in. thick slices. Place the lemon zest and juice in a bowl, add the oil and some salt and pepper. Place the courgette/zucchini slices in a shallow dish, pour over the dressing and stir well to coat. Leave to marinate for 30 minutes.

★ Preheat the oven to 150°C (300°F) Gas 3 and line a large baking sheet with baking parchment. Shred the kale into bite-sized pieces, discarding the thick stalks, and place in a bowl. Combine with the oil until the leaves are well coated. Scatter over the baking sheet and roast for 18–20 minutes until crisp. Season with salt and pepper and scatter with the sesame seeds.

★ Make the pesto. Toast the pumpkin seeds in a small frying pan/skillet over a medium heat for 2–3 minutes until golden. Cool and put in a food processor with the rocket/arugula, garlic, oil and a little salt and pepper. Blend until smooth.

★ Make the whipped feta. Place the ingredients in a blender and purée until really smooth.

★ Heat a ridged stovetop grill pan until hot and cook the courgette/zucchini slices for 2–3 minutes on each side until charred and tender. Cut the rolls in half and lightly toast the cut sides under the grill/broiler. Fill the rolls with the courgette/zucchini slices, whipped feta, pesto and some of the crispy kale. Serve at once with the remaining crispy kale on the side.

BEETROOT/BEETS BURGER
with wholegrain mustard mayonnaise

THERE IS NO QUESTION THAT REDUCING THE AMOUNT OF MEAT IN YOUR DIET IS NOT ONLY GOOD FOR YOUR HEALTH BUT ALSO FOR THE PLANET, SO HAVE A GO AT MAKING THIS VEGGIE BURGER. IT IS NOT AN ATTEMPT TO REPLICATE A BEEF BURGER, BUT IT IS VERY SIMILAR IN TEXTURE AND JUST AS SATISFYING.

a handful of fresh dill, finely chopped

a handful of fresh parsley, finely chopped

leaves from 2 sprigs of thyme

350 g/12 oz. beetroot/beets, grated

150 g/5 oz. carrot, finely grated

120 g/1 cup oatmeal

3 eggs

1 small red onion, finely chopped

2 garlic cloves, crushed

sea salt and freshly ground black pepper

1 tablespoon vegetable oil

slaw

½ small celeriac/celery root

½ red cabbage

2 carrots, shredded

1 red onion, thinly sliced

small handful of hazelnuts, toasted and chopped

3 tablespoons freshly chopped parsley

2 eating apples

3 tablespoons Mustard Mayo (see page 128), plus extra to serve

1 tablespoon extra virgin olive oil

zest of 1 lemon, plus juice of ½

to serve

10 bread rolls or pita bread

a handful of rocket/arugula and halved cherry tomatoes

makes 10

★ Thoroughly combine the herbs, beetroot/beets, carrot, oatmeal, eggs, onion and garlic in a bowl, making sure the eggs and herbs are evenly distributed. Season with 1 teaspoon salt and a few grindings of pepper. Set aside for 15 minutes.

★ Preheat the oven to 180°C (350°F) Gas 4.

★ To make the burgers, form 10 patties with your hands, squeezing the mixture together and shaping into burger patties. Press each burger down to make them nice and flat. Heat the vegetable oil in a frying pan/skillet over a low heat and fry the burgers until just browned – 2–3 minutes on each side. Transfer to an ovenproof dish and bake in the preheated oven for 20 minutes.

★ To make the slaw, cut the celeriac/celery root into thin matchsticks and slice the red cabbage very thinly. Combine with the carrots, onion, hazelnuts and most of the parsley in a bowl. When you are ready to serve the slaw, cut the apple into thin half-moon slices, getting rid of the core, and mix into the bowl. Add 3 tablespoons of the Mustard Mayo, the lemon zest and juice, ½ teaspoon salt and a pinch of pepper and mix well. Taste and if necessary, add a little extra salt, olive oil or wholegrain mustard.

★ Lightly toast the bread rolls or pita bread, if you like. Cut them open and spread the Mustard Mayo on the inside. Add the rocket/arugula, some halved tomatoes, some slaw and a burger. Serve at once.

250 g/9 oz. halloumi

1 tablespoon olive oil

8 small wholemeal/wholewheat baps

a handful of rocket/arugula leaves

8 baby tomatoes, halved

sweet chilli/chile jam

6 large red chillies/chiles, seeded and chopped

4 garlic cloves, chopped

1 teaspoon grated root ginger

1 teaspoon salt

100 ml/⅓ cup rice wine vinegar

100 g/½ cup granulated sugar

onion rings

125 g/1 cup plain/all-purpose flour

30 g/¼ cup cornflour/cornstarch

a pinch of salt

250 ml/1 cup sparkling water

1 onion, sliced into rings

sunflower oil, for frying

serves 4

STICKY SWEET CHILLI/ CHILE HALLOUMI SLIDERS
with crispy onion rings

- -

PARTNERING DELICIOUSLY SALTY HALLOUMI WITH A LITTLE SWEET CHILLI/CHILE JAM MAKES A KNOCKOUT COMBINATION. YOU CAN TEMPER THE HEAT OF THE CHILLI/CHILE JAM BY USING FEWER CHILLIES/CHILES IF YOU PREFER.

★ Preheat the oven to 180°C (350°F) Gas 4.

★ Make the jam. Place the chillies/chiles, garlic, ginger and salt in a food processor, blend to a rough paste and transfer to a saucepan. Add the vinegar and sugar, bring to the boil and simmer gently, partially covered, for 5–10 minutes, until the mixture thickens. Cool completely, pour into a sterilized jar and store in the refrigerator until needed.

★ Make the onion rings. Sift the flours into a bowl, add the salt and then gradually whisk in the water to make a smooth batter. Let sit for 10 minutes. Fill a wok or large heavy-bottomed saucepan with 5 cm/2 in. of sunflower oil and heat until a cube of bread added to the pan crisps immediately. Whisk the batter again, dip the onion rings in a few at a time and deep fry for 2–3 minutes until crisp and golden. Keep warm in the oven while cooking the halloumi.

★ Cut the halloumi into eight 3-mm/⅛-in. thick slices. Heat the oil in a frying pan/skillet over a high heat and fry the slices for 30 seconds on each side until starting to brown. Brush with a little of the Sweet Chilli/ Chile Jam and cook for a further 30 seconds on each side until golden and sticky.

★ Cut the rolls in half and lightly toast the cut sides under the grill/ broiler. Fill with the halloumi, rocket/arugula, tomato halves and the onion rings. Serve at once with a little extra Sweet Chilli/Chile Jam.

8 large portobello mushrooms

4–6 tablespoons olive oil

4 large burger buns, halved

4 tablespoons Sweet Chilli/Chile Jam (see page 71)

a handful of rocket/arugula

sea salt and freshly ground black pepper

caramelized garlic aïoli

1 large head garlic

2 egg yolks

1 teaspoon Dijon mustard

1 teaspoon freshly squeezed lemon juice

200 ml/1 cup olive oil

serves 4

GARLIC MUSHROOM BURGER
with caramelized aïoli

MUSHROOMS, WITH THEIR MEATY TEXTURE AND EARTHY FLAVOUR, PROVIDE VEGETARIANS WITH A GREAT MEAT-FREE ALTERNATIVE TO HAMBURGERS. HERE THEY ARE SERVED WITH A GARLIC SAUCE, BUT YOU CAN ALSO SERVE THEM TRADITIONALLY WITH MUSTARD, SALAD, CHEESE AND PICKLES.

★ Preheat the oven to 200°C (400°F) Gas 6.

★ To make the caramelized garlic aïoli, wrap the garlic head in foil and bake in the preheated oven for 45–50 minutes until the garlic is really soft. Let cool, then squeeze the garlic purée out of each clove into a bowl.

★ Put the egg yolks, mustard, lemon juice, salt and the garlic purée in a food processor and blend briefly until frothy. With the blade running, gradually pour in the oil through the funnel until the sauce is thickened and all the oil incorporated. Transfer the aïoli to a bowl, cover the surface with clingfilm/plastic wrap and chill until required.

★ Preheat the barbecue or grill/broiler. Peel the mushroom caps and trim the stalks so they are flat with the cups. Brush lightly with olive oil, season with salt and pepper and barbecue or grill/broil for 4–5 minutes on each side until softened and cooked through.

★ Lightly toast the buns under the grill/broiler and fill with the mushrooms, caramelized garlic aïoli, Sweet Chilli/Chile Jam and some rocket/arugula. Serve at once.

OPEN TOFU BEAN BURGER

TO ADD EXTRA FLAVOUR TO THESE BURGERS, LOOK OUT FOR THE VARIETIES OF TOFU THAT COME READY-MARINATED OR SMOKED. BOTH ARE READILY AVAILABLE FROM LARGER SUPERMARKETS AND HEALTH FOOD SHOPS.

2 tablespoons olive oil

1 onion, chopped

1 garlic clove, crushed

2 teaspoons ground coriander

1 teaspoon ground cumin

400 g/14 oz. canned red kidney beans, drained

200 g/8 oz. marinated or smoked tofu

75 g/1½ cups fresh wholemeal/wholewheat breadcrumbs

50 g/⅓ cup crunchy peanut butter

2 tablespoons chopped fresh coriander/cilantro

1 egg, lightly beaten

sea salt and freshly ground black pepper

plain/all-purpose flour, for dusting

peanut oil, for shallow frying

to serve

2 wholemeal/wholewheat burger buns, halved

a few fresh mint, basil and coriander/cilantro leaves

Sweet Chilli/chile Dressing (see page 38)

serves 4

★ Heat the olive oil in a frying pan/skillet, add the onion, garlic and spices and fry gently for 10 minutes until the onion is softened but not browned. Let cool. Transfer the onion mixture to a food processor, add the beans, tofu, breadcrumbs, peanut butter, coriander/cilantro, egg, salt and pepper and blend until smooth. Transfer the mixture to a bowl, cover and chill for 30 minutes.

★ Using wet hands, divide the mixture into eight portions and shape into burger patties. Press each burger down to make them nice and flat. Dust them lightly with flour. Heat a shallow layer of peanut oil in a frying pan/skillet, add the burgers and fry for 3–4 minutes on each side until crisp and heated through.

★ Lightly toast the buns under the grtill/broiler and top each half with two patties, fresh herbs and a drizzle of Sweet Chilli Dressing. Serve at once.

SPICED FALAFEL BURGER

with tahini yogurt sauce

- -

FALAFELS ARE EGYPTIAN BEAN PATTIES TRADITIONALLY SERVED IN PITA BREAD WITH SALAD LEAVES AND HUMMUS. HERE THEY MAKE A GREAT BURGER FILLING WITH A TANGY YOGURT DRESSING. TAHINI IS SESAME SEED PASTE AND IS AVAILABLE FROM SPECIALIST FOOD SHOPS.

225 g/1¼ cups dried chickpeas/garbanzo beans

1 small onion, finely chopped

2 garlic cloves, crushed

½ bunch of fresh flat-leaf parsley

½ bunch of fresh coriander/cilantro

2 teaspoons ground coriander

½ teaspoon baking powder

sea salt and freshly ground black pepper

sunflower or peanut oil, for shallow frying

tahini yogurt sauce

125 g/½ cup Greek-style yogurt

1 tablespoon tahini paste

1 garlic clove, crushed

½ tablespoon freshly squeezed lemon juice

1 tablespoon extra virgin olive oil

to serve

4 soft oval/hero rolls

a handful of salad leaves

2 tomatoes, diced

serves 4

★ Put the dried chickpeas/gabanzo beans in a bowl and add cold water to cover by at least 12 cm/5 in. Let soak overnight. Drain the chickpeas/beans well, transfer to a food processor and blend until coarsely ground. Add the onion, garlic, parsley, coriander/cilantro, ground coriander, baking powder and some salt and pepper and blend until very smooth. Transfer to a bowl, cover and chill for 30 minutes.

★ To make the tahini sauce, put the yogurt, tahini, garlic, lemon juice and olive oil in a bowl and whisk until smooth. Season to taste with salt and pepper and set aside until required.

★ Using wet hands, shape the chickpea mixture into 12 small or 8 medium burger patties. Press each patty down to make them nice and flat. Heat a shallow layer of oil in a frying pan/skillet, add the patties and fry for 3 minutes on each side until golden and cooked through. Drain on kitchen paper.

★ Cut the rolls in half and fill with 2–3 patties, tahini yogurt sauce, salad leaves and diced tomato. Serve at once.

CHUNKY AUBERGINE/EGGPLANT BURGERS

with pesto dressing

1 large aubergine/eggplant, about 750 g/1½ lb.

4 tablespoons extra virgin olive oil

1 tablespoon balsamic vinegar

1 garlic clove, crushed

sea salt and freshly ground black pepper

pesto

50 g/1½ cups fresh basil leaves

1 garlic clove, crushed

4 tablespoons pine nuts

7 tablespoons extra virgin olive oil

2 tablespoons freshly grated Parmesan cheese

to serve

4 soft bread rolls, halved

2 beefsteak tomatoes, thickly sliced

200 g/8 oz. mozzarella cheese, sliced

a handful of rocket/arugula

serves 4

THE SMOKY TASTE OF CHARGRILLED AUBERGINES/EGGPLANT AND THE BASIL PESTO GIVE THESE BURGERS A DISTINCTIVE MEDITERRANEAN FLAVOUR. YOU COULD REPLACE THE SLICED TOMATOES WITH SEMI-DRIED TOMATOES, IF YOU LIKE.

★ To make the pesto, put the basil, garlic, pine nuts, oil and some salt and pepper in a food processor and blend until fairly smooth. Transfer to a bowl, stir in the Parmesan and add more salt and pepper to taste. Set aside until required.

★ Preheat the grill/broiler to hot. Cut the aubergine/eggplant into 1-cm/½-in. slices. Put the oil, vinegar, garlic, salt and pepper in a bowl, whisk to mix, then brush over the aubergine/eggplant slices. Arrange them on a foil-lined grill pan and grill under the preheated grill/broiler for 3–4 minutes on each side until charred and softened.

★ Lightly toast the rolls under the grill/broiler and top with a slice of aubergine/eggplant. Spread with pesto, add another slice of aubergine/eggplant, then add a slice of tomato and mozzarella. Drizzle with more pesto, then top with a few rocket/arugula leaves. Put the tops on the rolls and serve at once.

RICE & BEAN BURGERS

200 g/1½ cups brown rice (not quick-cook variety)

2 tablespoons Worcestershire sauce

1 onion, chopped

2 garlic cloves, crushed

200-g/6½ oz. tin/canned cannellini beans, drained and rinsed

200-g/6½ oz. tin/canned red kidney beans, drained and rinsed

50 g/½ cup breadcrumbs

1 egg, beaten

115 g/1 cup Cheddar cheese, grated

2 tablespoons freshly chopped thyme

1 small green (bell) pepper, deseeded and chopped

1 large carrot, coarsely grated·

flour or cornflour/cornmeal, for coating

2–3 tablespoons sunflower oil

salt and freshly ground black pepper

salad leaves and relish, to serve (optional)

makes 10

THIS VERSATILE RECIPE CAN EASILY BE ADAPTED WITH DIFFERENT FLAVOURINGS. FOR EXAMPLE, ADD 1–2 DESEEDED FINELY CHOPPED CHILLIES/CHILES FOR EXTRA HEAT OR 3 FINELY CHOPPED CELERY STALKS FOR ADDED CRUNCH, OR REPLACE THE THYME WITH FRESHLY CHOPPED CORIANDER/CILANTRO.

★ Cook the rice according to the instructions on the packet, allowing it to slightly overcook so that it is soft. Drain the rice, transfer it to a large bowl and reserve.

★ Put 2 tablespoons water and the Worcestershire sauce in a frying pan/skillet, add the onion and garlic and cook for about 8 minutes over a medium heat until softened.

★ Put the onion, garlic, cooked rice, beans, breadcrumbs, egg, cheese and thyme in a blender or food processor. Add plenty of salt and pepper, then blend until combined. Alternatively, you can mash everything roughly in a bowl with a potato masher. Add the green pepper and grated carrot and mix well. Refrigerate the mixture for 1½ hours, or until quite firm.

★ Shape the mixture into 10 burger patties, using wet hands if the mixture sticks. Press each burger down to make them nice and flat. Coat them in flour or cornflour/cornmeal and refrigerate for a further 30 minutes.

★ Heat the oil in a frying pan/skillet and fry the burgers for 3–4 minutes on each side, or until piping hot. Serve with salad leaves and relish.

MIDDLE EASTERN SLIDERS
with tahini sauce

LOVELY RICH FLAVOURS COMBINE IN THIS MIDDLE EASTERN-STYLE DISH, WHERE AUBERGINE/EGGPLANT IS PARTNERED WITH PRESERVED LEMON, POMEGRANATE, TAHINI AND RAS EL HANOUT – A CLASSIC SPICE MIX.

100 g/3½ oz. semi-dried tomatoes, sliced

½ preserved lemon, flesh discarded and skin diced

4 tablespoons pine nuts

4 tablespoons pomegranate seeds

4 tablespoons parsley leaves

3 tablespoons extra virgin olive oil

2 teaspoons honey

1 large aubergine/eggplant (about 450 g/1 lb.)

1 teaspoon ras el hanout

salt and freshly ground black pepper

tahini sauce

100 g/⅓ cup Greek yogurt

2 tablespoons tahini paste

1 small garlic clove, crushed

1 tablespoon freshly squeezed lemon juice

to serve

8 small ciabatta rolls

a handful of salad leaves

serves 4

★ In a bowl, combine the semi-dried tomatoes, preserved lemon, pine nuts, pomegranate seeds, parsley, 2 tablespoons of the oil, the honey and some salt and pepper. Set aside.

★ Cut the aubergine/eggplant widthways into 8 thick slices. Combine 2 tablespoons of the remaining oil with the ras el hanout and some salt and pepper and brush over the slices.

★ Heat a ridged stovetop grill pan until hot and griddle the aubergine/eggplant for 4–5 minutes on each side until well charred and softened.

★ Meanwhile, beat together the yogurt, tahini, garlic and lemon juice and season to taste.

★ To serve, cut the rolls in half and lightly toast the cut sides under the grill/broiler. Fill with the aubergine/eggplant slices, tomato mixture, tahini sauce and salad leaves. Serve at once.

CURRIED SWEET POTATO BURGERS

YOU CAN EITHER ADD SOME LIME PICKLE AND NATURAL YOGURT TO THESE NUTTY BURGERS OR SERVE THEM ROLLED IN WARM CHAPATTI BREAD. BULGHUR IS A CRACKED WHEAT AND IS AVAILABLE FROM SUPERMARKETS AND HEALTH FOOD SHOPS.

75 g/½ cup bulghur wheat

400 g/1 lb. sweet potatoes, cubed

1½ tablespoons olive oil, plus extra for shallow frying

1 small onion, finely chopped

1 garlic clove, crushed

1 tablespoon curry powder

75 g/½ cup blanched almonds, finely chopped

2 tablespoons chopped fresh coriander/cilantro

1 egg, lightly beaten

4 tablespoons chickpea flour or plain/all-purpose flour

sea salt and freshly ground black pepper

to serve

4 burger buns/herbed rolls/chapatti bread

a handful of salad leaves

sliced cucumber

4 tablespoons mango chutney

lime pickle

plain yogurt

serves 4

★ Put the bulghur wheat in a heatproof bowl, add boiling water to cover by 3 cm/1 in. and set aside to soak for 20 minutes until tender. Drain well.

★ Meanwhile, steam the sweet potatoes for 10–15 minutes until cooked. Drain well and mash with a potato masher.

★ Heat the olive oil in a frying pan/skillet and fry the onion, garlic and curry powder for 10 minutes until the onion is softened.

★ Put the bulghur wheat, mashed sweet potato, onion mixture, almonds, coriander/cilantro, egg, flour and some salt and pepper in a bowl. Work together with your hands until evenly mixed. Cover and chill for 30 minutes. Using wet hands, divide the mixture into eight portions and shape into burger patties. Press each burger down to make them nice and flat.

★ Heat a shallow layer of olive oil in a frying pan/skillet, add the patties and fry gently for 3–4 minutes on each side until golden and heated through. Lightly toast the buns under the grill/broiler and fill with the patties, salad leaves, cucumber slices and mango chutney. Top with some lime pickle and yogurt, if using, and serve at once.

QUINOA BURGERS WITH PORTOBELLO MUSHROOMS

- -

HERE MOIST QUINOA MIXES BEAUTIFULLY WITH SWEET POTATO AND BLACK BEANS TO GIVE A HEARTY CONSISTENCY. THIS BURGER WILL SATISFY MEAT-EATERS AS WELL AS VEGETARIANS.

3 tablespoons olive oil

1 onion, finely chopped

2 garlic cloves, crushed

75 g/½ cup black beans

120 g/1 cup cooked quinoa (see Note)

100 g/½ cup cooked sweet potato, flesh scooped out

1 carrot, shredded

½ teaspoon ground cumin

½ teaspoon ground coriander

2 tablespoons freshly chopped parsley

1 tablespoon breadcrumbs

5 portobello mushrooms

a pinch each of sea salt and freshly ground black pepper

to serve

1 avocado, sliced

1 large tomato, sliced

1 gherkin/pickle, chopped

½ red onion, sliced

a handful of fresh coriander/cilantro

1–2 tablespoons freshly squeezed lime juice

a baking sheet, lined with baking parchment

makes 5

★ Preheat the oven to 180°C (350°F) Gas 4.

★ Heat 1 tablespoon of the olive oil in a saucepan or pot over a medium heat. Fry the onion for about 3 minutes, until softened. Add the garlic and cook for another minute. Add the beans, stir and cook for a few minutes longer. Remove from the heat and transfer the mixture to a large mixing bowl.

★ Lightly mash the beans with a fork until they are semi-crushed. Add the rest of the ingredients (except the mushrooms and remaining olive oil) to the bowl and mix well. If the mixture is too moist, add extra breadcrumbs. If too dry, add some more smashed beans.

★ Work the mixture together with your hands until evenly mixed. Divide the mixture into five portions and shape into burger patties. Press each burger down to make them nice and flat. Place on the prepared baking sheet and bake in the preheated oven for 20–25 minutes, turning once to ensure even browning. Remove from the oven and keep warm.

★ Increase the oven to 200°C (400°F) Gas 6. Clean the mushrooms with a damp cloth. Remove the stems and drizzle with the remaining 2 tablespoons olive oil. Season with salt and pepper and roast in the oven for 20 minutes.

★ To serve, place each burger on top of a roasted mushroom and garnish with your choice of burger toppings. Serve at once.

Note: To prepare quinoa, put 210 g/1 cup quinoa in a frying pan/skillet with 240 ml/1 cup stock and 200 ml/1 cup water. Bring to the boil, then reduce the heat, cover and simmer for 20 minutes. Uncover, fluff with a fork and set aside for 5 minutes before using.

MUSHROOM BURGERS
with chilli/chile mayonnaise & onion pickle

1 fresh hot red chilli/chile, about 5 cm/2 in. long

about 120 ml/½ cup Classic Mayo (see page 128)

2 tablespoons extra virgin olive oil

4 large portobello mushrooms, stems trimmed

4 hamburger buns, split in half

a handful of salad leaves

sea salt and freshly ground black pepper

onion pickle

2 tablespoons olive oil

2 red onions, thinly sliced

60 ml/¼ cup redcurrant jelly

1 tablespoon red wine vinegar

serves 4

JUST THE TICKET FOR PEOPLE WHO DON'T EAT MEAT BUT LOVE A GOOD BURGER. THE ONION PICKLE CAN BE MADE AHEAD AND KEPT IN THE REFRIGERATOR FOR SEVERAL DAYS.

★ To make the onion pickle, heat the oil in a saucepan, add the onions, and sauté gently for 15 minutes or until very soft. Add a pinch of salt, the redcurrant jelly, vinegar and 2 tablespoons water and cook for 15 minutes more, or until the mixture is glossy and thickened. Let cool.

★ Preheat a ridged stovetop grill pan, then cook the chilli/chile whole for 1–2 minutes, or until the skin is charred and blackened. Transfer to a sealable plastic bag, seal and let cool slightly. Peel the chilli/chile, then remove and discard the seeds. Chop the flesh and transfer to a food processor. Add the mayonnaise and process until the sauce is speckled red. Taste and adjust the seasoning with salt and pepper, if necessary.

★ Brush the olive oil over the mushrooms, season well with salt and pepper, and cook in the grill pan, stem-side down, for 5 minutes. Using a spatula, flip the mushrooms and cook them on the other side for about 5 minutes, until they are tender.

★ Lightly toast the split buns under the grill/broiler, then fill them with the mushrooms, salad leaves, onion pickle and a spoonful of the chilli/chile mayonnaise.

CHEESY ROOT VEGETABLE BURGER with mustard mayo

⅓ butternut squash, peeled and chopped

1 sweet potato, peeled and chopped

1 small potato, peeled and chopped

1 carrot, peeled and chopped

½ red onion, chopped

1 garlic clove, chopped

a large pinch of dried thyme

40 g/⅓ cup grated mature/sharp Cheddar cheese

a pinch of sea salt and freshly ground black pepper

to serve

Mustard Mayo (see page 128)

a handful of salad leaves

serves 2

THESE HEARTY VEGETARIAN BURGERS DON'T REQUIRE A BUN BECAUSE THEY ARE PACKED FULL OF YUMMY ROOT VEGETABLES. SERVE WITH MUSTARD MAYO AND SALAD LEAVES.

★ Bring a large saucepan of water to the boil. Put in the squash, sweet potato, potato, carrot, onion and garlic and boil for about 10 minutes until soft. Strain and mash well with a potato masher. Add the thyme and salt and pepper and work together with your hands until evenly mixed.

★ Divide the mixture in half and shape into two burger patties. Press each burger down to make them nice and flat, then roll each one in the cheese, so that it sticks all around the outside of the burger.

★ Preheat the grill/broiler to medium–hot.

★ Put the burgers on a greased baking sheet and and grill/broil for 6–8 minutes on each side until the cheese is brown and bubbling. Let cool slightly before serving.

★ Serve with Mustard Mayo and a mixed leaf salad.

340 g/12 oz. lean minced/ground beef

1 tablespoon olive or vegetable oil

a large pinch of sea salt and freshly ground black pepper

tomato relish

1 tablespoon olive oil

1 onion, sliced

1 garlic clove, crushed

1 fresh red chilli/chile, chopped

800 g/3½ cups canned chopped tomatoes

200 ml/¾ cup red wine vinegar

200 g/1 cup sugar

30 g/3 tablespoons capers, rinsed

3 or 4 baby gherkins, chopped

a handful of fresh coriander/cilantro

sea salt and freshly ground black pepper

to serve

2 slices of bacon

4 slices of Cheddar cheese

2 large burger buns

butter, for spreading

2 tablespoons American mustard

2 pickled gherkins, thinly sliced

a handful of lettuce, chopped

Classic Homecut Fries (see page 125)

serves 2

ULTIMATE BACON-CHEESE BURGER with tomato relish

WHY GO TO A RESTAURANT WHEN YOU CAN MAKE THESE DELICIOUS GOURMET BURGERS AT HOME? THIS EASY RECIPE COMBINES A TASTY BEEF PATTY WITH ALL THE TRIMMINGS.

★ To make the tomato relish, heat the oil in a frying pan/skillet set over a medium heat. Add the onion, garlic and chilli/chile and fry, stirring occasionally, until soft. Add the tomatoes and mix well. Add the vinegar and sugar and bring to the boil. Reduce the heat and simmer for 30 minutes. Season with salt and pepper, to taste. The relish should be the consistency of jam. Take off the heat and stir in the capers, gherkins and coriander/cilantro. Taste and adjust the seasoning, if necessary. Set aside to cool.

★ To make the burgers, put the beef in a bowl with the salt and pepper. Work together with your hands until evenly mixed. Divide the beef mixture in half and shape into two burger patties. Press each burger down to make them nice and flat.

★ Heat the oil in a frying pan/skillet and fry the burgers over a medium–high heat for 5 minutes on each side until cooked through.

★ Meanwhile, heat a separate frying pan/skillet until hot and fry the bacon slices until crisp. Remove from the pan and set aside.

★ When the burgers are cooked, remove from the pan and top each with two slices of cheese. Set aside to allow the cheese to melt slightly.

★ Slice the burger buns in half and lightly toast them under the grill/broiler.

★ Spread butter on the cut sides of each bun. Squeeze a little mustard onto the base and put the cooked burgers on top. Add a generous spoonful of tomato relish to each and top with the bacon, gherkins and lettuce. Finish the burgers with the lids of the buns and serve with Classic Homecut Fries.

DEEP-FRIED BUTTERMILK CHICKEN BURGER with 'nduja & slaw

8 skinless chicken thigh fillets

250 ml/1 cup buttermilk

sunflower oil, for frying

4 brioche burger buns

125 g/4½ oz. 'nduja sausage

a handful of lettuce leaves

slaw

125 g/2 cups red cabbage, shredded

100 g/¾ cup carrots, grated

½ red onion, thinly sliced

1 teaspoon sea salt

1½ teaspoons sugar

2 teaspoons white wine vinegar

6 tablespoons Classic Mayo (see page 128)

coating

100 g/¾ cup plain/all-purpose flour

1 teaspoon sea salt

1 teaspoon mustard powder

½ teaspoon smoked paprika

½ teaspoon celery salt

¼ teaspoon freshly ground black pepper

serves 4

'NDUJA IS A TYPE OF ITALIAN SALAMI BLENDED WITH ROASTED RED PEPPERS INTO A SPICY PASTE. IF YOU ARE UNABLE TO FIND IT, YOU CAN SIMPLY BLEND SOME CHORIZO SAUSAGE IN A FOOD PROCESSOR UNTIL IT IS PASTE-LIKE, WHICH MAKES FOR A DECENT ALTERNATIVE.

★ Cut the chicken thigh fillets in half and place in a shallow dish. Pour over the buttermilk, cover and chill overnight. This will tenderize the chicken. The next day, remove the chicken from the fridge and return to room temperature for 30 minutes.

★ Make the slaw. Combine the cabbage, carrots and onion with the salt, sugar and vinegar and set aside for 30 minutes. Drain the cabbage mixture and combine with the mayonnaise.

★ Make the coating mix. In a bowl, combine the flour, salt, mustard powder, smoked paprika, celery salt and black pepper.

★ Carefully remove the chicken thighs from the buttermilk and immediately dip into the flour mixture, making sure they are completely coated.

★ Preheat the oven to 180°C (350°F) Gas 4.

★ Heat 5 cm/2 inches of sunflower oil in a saucepan until hot and a cube of bread dropped into the oil crisps in 20 seconds. Deep-fry the coated chicken pieces for 3–4 minutes on each side until crisp and golden. Transfer them to the oven to keep warm while cooking the rest.

★ To serve, cut the buns in half and lightly toast the cut sides under the grill/broiler. Fill with the chicken fritters and add some 'nduja, lettuce and slaw. Serve at once, with sweet potato wedges, if you like.

BIG BREAKFAST BURGER
with mushroom & fried egg

A HEARTY PORK BURGER WITH ALL THE TRADITIONAL BREAKFAST TRIMMINGS – FOR THOSE MORNINGS WHEN A SIMPLE BOWL OF CEREAL JUST WON'T CUT IT.

2 tablespoons olive oil

5 mushrooms, finely chopped

200 g/7 oz. lean minced/ground pork

2 teaspoons Homemade Tomato Ketchup (see page 127), plus extra to serve

a pinch of mustard powder

3 tablespoons fresh breadcrumbs

a pinch of sea salt and freshly ground black pepper

to serve

2 English muffins

2 fried eggs

2 grilled/broiled Portobello mushrooms

serves 2

★ Heat 1 tablespoon of the oil in a frying pan/skillet over a medium heat. Add the chopped mushrooms and fry until soft and brown. Remove from the pan and set aside.

★ Put the pork in a bowl with the tomato ketchup, mustard powder, breadcrumbs and salt and pepper. Work together with your hands until evenly mixed. Add the cooled mushrooms and mix again. Divide the mixture in half and shape into two burger patties. Press each burger down to make them nice and flat.

★ Heat the remaining oil in the same frying pan/skillet and fry the burgers over a medium–high heat for 5 minutes on each side until cooked through.

★ Slice the English muffins in half and lightly toast them under the grill/broiler or in the toaster. Spread a spoonful of Homemade Tomato Ketchup on the base of each muffin and put the cooked burgers on top. Put a fried egg and a grilled/broiled Portobello mushroom on top of each burger and finish with the lids of the English muffins. Serve at once with extra Homemade Tomato Ketchup on the side.

TRIPLE WHAMMY BRUNCH BURGER

750 g /1½ lb. minced/ground beef

1 onion, finely chopped

1 tablespoon wholegrain mustard

4 slices of smoked back bacon

4 plum tomatoes, sliced

4 eggs

sea salt and freshly ground black pepper

olive oil, for brushing

peanut or sunflower oil, for shallow frying

to serve

4 English muffins, halved

Homemade Tomato Ketchup, to serve (see page 127)

serves 4

THIS SUBSTANTIAL MULTI-LAYERED BURGER IS THE PERFECT THING TO SERVE FOR A LAZY WEEKEND BRUNCH. ENJOY WITH FRESHLY SQUEEZED ORANGE JUICE AND MUGS OF COFFEE ON THE SIDE.

★ Put the beef, onion, mustard and some salt and pepper in a bowl and work together with your hands until evenly mixed and slightly sticky. Divide into four portions and shape into burger patties. Press each burger down to make them nice and flat. Cover and chill for 30 minutes.

★ Brush the patties lightly with olive oil and pan-grill for 4–5 minutes on each side until cooked through. Keep them warm.

★ Meanwhile, heat a frying pan/skillet until hot and dry-fry the bacon for 2–3 minutes on each side until crisp. Keep it warm with the burgers. Add the tomatoes to the pan and fry for 2 minutes on each side, keep warm with the burgers and bacon.

★ Heat a shallow layer of peanut or sunflower oil in the frying pan/skillet, add the eggs and fry for 2–3 minutes or until cooked to your liking.

★ Toast the muffins under the grill/broiler or in the toaster. Put the tomato slices on the bases, followed by the burgers, bacon and fried eggs. Spoon over some Homemade Tomato Ketchup and add the muffin tops. Serve at once.

HAWAIIAN TERIYAKI PORK BURGER with pineapple rings & avocado mayonnaise

2 tablespoons soy sauce

2 tablespoon sake

1 tablespoon mirin

1 teaspoon caster/granulated sugar

15 g/1 tablespoon butter

500 g/1 lb. 2oz. minced/ground pork

1 tablespoon freshly chopped coriander/cilantro leaves

4 sesame seed burger rolls

a handful of salad leaves

pineapple rings

1 small pineapple

1 tablespoon olive oil

1 tablespoon agave syrup

2 tablespoons white wine vinegar

¼ teaspoon ground cinnamon

avocado mayonnaise

1 avocado, peeled and stoned

2 tablespoons Classic Mayo (see page 128)

1 teaspoon wasabi paste

juice of ½ lime

salt and freshly ground black pepper

serves 4

HAWAIIAN FOOD TAKES ITS INSPIRATION FROM MANY DIFFERENT CUISINES, INCLUDING JAPANESE, MEXICAN AND AMERICAN, AND THESE FLAVOURS COMBINE BEAUTIFULLY IN THIS COLOURFUL BURGER. AGAVE SYRUP (FOR THE PINEAPPLE RINGS) CAN BE READILY REPLACED BY HONEY IF YOU WISH.

★ Make the burgers. Place the soy sauce, sake, mirin, sugar and butter in a small saucepan and simmer gently for 2–3 minutes until reduced by half and sticky. Let cool. Combine the pork with the coriander/cilantro and 1½ tablespoons of the soy mixture (reserving the rest) and work together with your hands to form a sticky mixture. Divide the mixture into four portions and shape into burger patties. Press each burger down to make them nice and flat. Cover and chill for 30 minutes.

★ Meanwhile, prepare the pineapple rings. Peel the skin from the pineapple, cut into 5-mm/¼-inch thick slices and using a small pastry cutter, cut out the central core. Combine the oil, agave syrup and a pinch of salt in a small bowl and brush over the pineapple rings. Heat a frying pan/skillet over a medium heat and fry the rings for 2 minutes on each side until golden brown. Transfer to a bowl and add the vinegar and cinnamon, stir well and set aside.

★ Make the avocado mayonnaise. Dice the avocado flesh and place in a blender with the mayonnaise, wasabi and lime juice and purée until really smooth. Season to taste.

★ Heat a ridged stovetop grill pan over a medium heat. Brush the burgers with a little oil and griddle for 5 minutes on each side until charred and cooked through. Rest for 5 minutes.

★ To serve, cut the rolls in half and toast the cut sides under the grill/broiler. Put a layer of salad leaves on the base and top with the burgers, pineapple rings, avocado mayonnaise and the remaining teriyaki sauce mixture, warming it through again, if necessary. Top with the roll lids and serve at once.

BARBECUE BURGER

with crispy onion rings

PORK BELLY ADDS EXTRA FLAVOUR AND FAT TO THESE BEEF PATTIES, KEEPING THEM BEAUTIFULLY MOIST AS THEY COOK. CHOOSE GOOD-QUALITY, FLAVOURSOME MEAT.

650 g/1½ lb. chuck steak, coarsely chopped

100 g/4 oz. skinless pork belly, coarsely chopped

50 g/1 cup fresh white breadcrumbs

1 egg, lightly beaten

a few drops of Tabasco sauce

sea salt and freshly ground black pepper

olive oil, for brushing

crispy onion rings

1 onion, thinly sliced into rings

150 ml/⅔ cup milk

2 tablespoons plain/all-purpose flour, seasoned with salt and pepper

peanut or sunflower oil, for deep-frying

to serve

4 oval burger buns/hero rolls

a handful of baby spinach leaves

2 tomatoes, sliced

4 tablespoons Hot & Smoky Barbecue Sauce (see page 126)

serves 4

★ Put the beef and pork in a food processor and blend briefly until just minced. Transfer to a bowl and add the breadcrumbs, egg, Tabasco, salt and pepper and work together with your hands until evenly mixed and slightly sticky. Cover and chill for 30 minutes, then shape into eight small patties. Press each patty down to make them nice and flat.

★ Meanwhile, soak the onion rings in the milk for 30 minutes.

★ Brush the patties lightly with olive oil and barbecue or grill/broil for 3 minutes on each side until lightly charred and cooked through. Keep them warm.

★ Drain the soaked onion rings and dust with seasoned flour. Heat 5 cm/ 2 inches of peanut or sunflower oil in a deep, heavy saucepan until it reaches 180°C (350°F) on a cook's thermometer. Add the onion rings, in batches, and deep-fry for 2–3 minutes until crisp and golden. Drain on paper towels. Alternatively, use an electric deep-fryer and follow the manufacturer's instructions.

★ Slice the buns almost in half, open out and toast lightly on both sides under the grill/broiler or in a toaster. Fill the buns with spinach leaves, tomato slices, 2 patties and the Hot & Smoky Barbecue Sauce. Serve at once, topped with the crispy onion rings.

DINER CHEESEBURGER

450 g/1 lb. minced/ground beef

140 g/1 cup onion, minced

2 garlic cloves, pressed

8 slices of maple-cured bacon or regular bacon

sea salt and freshly ground black pepper

4 eggs

Dijonnaise

2 large white onions

2 tablespoons butter

400 ml/1¾ cups single/light cream

3 tablespoons Dijon mustard

pinch of salt, ground black pepper, garlic, nutmeg, chopped fresh flat-leaf parsley and tarragon

to serve

4 brioche buns

4 slices of American or Cheddar cheese

1 spicy dill pickle, chopped

Classic Homecut Fries (see page 125), to serve

ranch dressing

Onion Pickle (see page 84), to serve, optional

serves 4

ACCORDING TO FOOD HISTORIANS, THE CHEESEBURGER WAS INVENTED IN 1920 IN PASADENA, CALIFORNIA, A REMARKABLE 20 YEARS AFTER THE HAMBURGER FIRST APPEARED. LIONEL STERNBERGER (NO PUN INTENDED), A COOK AT HIS FATHER'S SANDWICH SHOP, 'THE RITE SPOT', ONE DAY DECIDED TO PLACE A SLAB OF AMERICAN CHEESE ON TOP OF A HAMBURGER, INVENTING ONE OF THE WORLD'S MOST LOVED DISHES.

★ First, make the Dijonnaise by finely chopping the white onions and frying with the butter in a medium saucepan. Add the cream and mix in the mustard. Season the mixture and simmer until the sauce takes a mustardy colour and is relatively thick.

★ Using your hands, mix together the minced/ground beef, minced onion and pressed garlic. Shape into 4 burger patties. Press each burger down to make them nice and flat. Sprinkle with salt and pepper. Grill/broil to your liking.

★ In a medium frying pan/skillet, fry the bacon and set aside. Fry the eggs in the same pan and set aside.

★ Cut the brioche buns in half and spread a layer of Dijonnaise. Place a burger on top, then a slice of cheese, followed by a fried egg, 2 slices of bacon and some chopped dill pickle.

★ Serve with Classic Homecut Fries, ranch dressing and Onion Pickle on the side, if you wish.

ROAST GARLIC PORK BURGER

½ teaspoon fennel seeds

1 roasted head of garlic (see page 72)

400 g/14 oz. minced/ground pork

1 tablespoon finely chopped fresh parsley

1 teaspoon grated lemon zest

sunflower or vegetable oil, for frying

salt and freshly ground black pepper

to serve

4 brioche rolls or hamburger buns

a handful of Little Gem lettuce leaves

Classic Mayo (see page 128), Homemade Tomato Ketchup (see page 127) and sliced gherkins, as desired

Classic Coleslaw (see page 130)

serves 4

MAKING YOUR OWN BURGERS ALLOWS YOU TO BE CREATIVE WITH THE FLAVOURINGS. ADDING ROAST GARLIC, FENNEL SEEDS AND LEMON ZEST GIVES A GREAT DEPTH OF FLAVOUR TO THESE TASTY BURGERS, PERFECT FOR SUMMERTIME BARBECUES. SERVE WITH A DISH OF CRUNCHY COLESLAW ON THE SIDE.

★ Dry-fry the fennel seeds in a frying pan/skillet until fragrant, then cool and grind.

★ When the roasted garlic is cool enough to handle, squeeze out the softened pulp from each clove and mash into a paste.

★ Put the minced/ground pork in a bowl with the roast garlic paste, ground fennel, parsley and lemon zest. Season well with salt and pepper and work together with your hands until evenly mixed. Divide the mixture into four portions and shape into burger patties. Press each burger down to make them nice and flat.

★ Add a touch of oil to a large frying pan/skillet and heat through. Add the patties and fry for 15–20 minutes, or until cooked through, turning over as they cook.

★ Place the patties in the rolls with a few lettuce leaves, adding Classic Mayo, Homemade Tomato Ketchup and gherkins to taste, and serve at once with Classic Coleslaw on the side.

PORK & CIDER BURGER

with blue cheese & asparagus

----

15 g/1 tablespoon butter

6 asparagus spears, sliced down the middle

190 g/6½ oz. lean minced/ground pork

30 g/1½ tablespoons crumbled firm blue cheese (such as Roquefort, Gorgonzola or Stilton)

3 tablespoons (hard) cider

4 teaspoons tomato purée/paste

1 tablespoon olive or vegetable oil

a pinch of sea salt and freshly ground black pepper

to serve

2 seeded wholemeal/wholewheat bread rolls

Classic Mayo (see page 128)

serves 2

THE SWEETNESS OF THE CIDER COMBINED WITH THE BLUE CHEESE ADDS A REAL DEPTH OF FLAVOUR TO THIS SUMPTUOUS PORK BURGER. IT IS EVEN MORE DELICIOUS SERVED WITH CREAMY HOMEMADE CLASSIC MAYO.

★ Heat the butter in a frying pan/skillet or ridged stovetop griddle pan set over high heat. Put the asparagus cut-side down in the pan and cook for a couple of minutes. Turn over and brown the other side. Remove from the pan and set aside.

★ Put the pork in a bowl with the blue cheese, cider, tomato purée/paste and salt and pepper. Work together with your hands until evenly mixed. Divide the mixture in half and shape into two burger patties. Press each burger down to make them nice and flat.

★ Heat the oil in the same frying pan/skillet and fry the burgers over a medium–high heat for 5 minutes on each side until cooked through.

★ Cut the bread rolls in half. Spread a spoonful of Classic Mayo on the bottom half of each roll and put the cooked burgers on top. Lay half the asparagus spears over the top of each burger. Finish with the lids of the bread rolls and serve at once.

PULLED PORK PRETZEL BUN BURGER

2 medium yellow onions, thinly sliced

4 medium garlic cloves, thinly sliced

120 ml/½ cup apple cider vinegar

120 ml/½ cup India pale ale

1 fresh sage leaf

1 tablespoon packed dark brown sugar

1 tablespoon chilli/chili powder

1 tablespoon sea salt, plus more as needed

1 teaspoon freshly ground black pepper

½ teaspoon ground cumin

¼ teaspoon ground cinnamon

1 (2¼ kg/5 lbs.) boneless or bone-in pork shoulder, twine or netting removed

to serve

350 g/1½ cups Hot & Smoky Barbecue Sauce (see page 126), optional

6 pretzel buns

butter, for spreading

Classic Coleslaw (see page 130)

slow cooker

serves 6

PULLED PORK BUNS ARE THE BEST THING TO MAKE WITH PORK SHOULDER AND IT TAKES VERY LITTLE WORK TO CREATE A DELICIOUS SLOW-COOKED BURGER FILLING. THE SECRET IS THE ADDITION OF INDIA PALE ALE (IPA) AND APPLE CIDER VINEGAR TO MAKE THE SAUCE.

★ Place the onions and garlic in an even layer in the slow cooker, pour in the vinegar and beer and add the sage leaf.

★ Combine the sugar, chilli/chili powder, salt, pepper, cumin and cinnamon in a small bowl. Pat the pork dry with paper towels. Rub the spice mixture all over the pork and place on top of the onions and garlic. Cover and cook until the pork is tender, about 6–8 hours on a high setting or 8–10 hours on low.

★ Turn off the slow cooker and move the pork to a cutting board. Set a fine-mesh sieve/strainer over a medium heatproof bowl. Pour the onion mixture from the slow cooker through the sieve/strainer and return the solids to the slow cooker. Set the strained liquid aside and use a spoon to skim and discard any fat from the surface.

★ If the pork has a bone, remove and discard it. Using two forks, shred the pork, discarding any large pieces of fat. Return the shredded meat to the slow cooker and add the barbecue sauce, if using, and mix to combine. Add 60 ml/¼ cup of the strained liquid at a time to the slow cooker until the pork is just moistened. Taste and season with salt as needed.

★ Cut each pretzel bun in half and butter the bottom. Lay a generous helping of pork onto each bun, spoon over the Hot & Smoky Barbecue Sauce and top with Classic Coleslaw, if using.

BURNT ENDS BURGER

THIS BURGER IS A GREAT WAY TO USE UP 'BURNT ENDS' – THESE ARE THE PIECES OF MEAT CUT FROM THE NARROWER END OF BEEF BRISKET. THE HIGH FAT CONTENT OF THE BRISKET POINT TAKES LONGER TO COOK TO TENDER, HENCE THE TERM 'BURNT ENDS'. YOU COULD ALSO USE LEFTOVER ROAST BEEF – THE WELL DONE ENDS OF A LARGE JOINT ARE IDEAL. THIS RECIPE USES A SMOKER – IT'S WELL WORTH TRYING THIS METHOD OF COOKING AS IT ADDS AN EXTRA LEVEL OF FLAVOUR TO FOOD.

450 g/1 lb. leftover cooked beef brisket (or roast beef)

125–250 ml/½–1 cup Hot & Smoky Barbecue Sauce (see page 126), plus extra to serve

125 ml/½ cup drippings from the brisket (or roast beef) roasting pan

to serve

4 pretzel buns

Sweet Potato Wedges (see page 124)

food smoker or barbecue

serves 4

★ Cut the leftover brisket or roast beef into 1.25-cm/½-inch cubes and place in a large disposable tray. Add in the Hot & Smoky Barbecue Sauce and any drippings from the roasting pan. Toss thoroughly.

★ Prepare a smoker following the manufacturer's instructions. If you haven't got a smoker, use a barbecue smoker box and fill it with wood chips that have been soaked in water or fruit juice for a couple of hours. Place the smoker box directly into a lit charcoal or gas barbecue.

★ Place the tray of meat in the smoker or barbecue and smoke at 100°C (225°F) until the meat darkens and becomes crisp around the edges – this will take 30–45 minutes.

★ Remove from the smoker or barbecue, and set aside to cool for 10 minutes.

★ Serve in the pretzel buns with additional barbecue sauce, if desired, alongside Sweet Potato Wedges.

CAJUN SALMON, DILL & CREME FRAICHE SLIDERS

350 g/12 oz. salmon fillets

1 garlic clove, crushed

2 teaspoons Cajun spice mix

2 spring onions/scallions, trimmed and chopped

100 g/3½ oz. smoked salmon

salt and freshly ground black pepper

sunflower oil, for frying

onion pickles

½ red onion

2 teaspoons white wine vinegar

1 teaspoon caster/granulated sugar

½ teaspoon salt

to serve

100 g/½ cup crème fraîche/sour cream

1 tablespoon freshly chopped dill

8 plain mini bagels

a handful of lettuce leaves

8 cornichons, sliced

makes 8

LOUISIANA, THE CAPITAL OF CAJUN COOKING, IS A MELTING POT OF CULTURES, REPRESENTED HERE WITH CAJUN SPICES COMBINED WITH NEW YORK DELI-STYLE PICKLED RED ONION RINGS, CORNICHONS AND CRÈME FRAÎCHE WITH DILL IN A BAGEL. IT MAKES A PERFECT POSH BRUNCH BURGER.

★ Make the onion pickles. Slice the red onion into rings and place in a bowl with the vinegar, sugar and salt. Soak for 1 hour, then rinse and pat dry.

★ Combine the salmon, garlic, Cajun spice mix, spring onions/scallions and some black pepper and blitz in a food processor. Chop the smoked salmon into small dice and stir through the puréed salmon mixture. Divide into eight portions and shape into slider patties. Press each slider down to make them nice and flat. Chill for 30 minutes.

★ Combine the crème fraîche and dill in a small bowl and season to taste.

★ Heat a shallow layer of oil in a large frying pan/skillet over a medium heat and fry the patties in batches for 3 minutes on each side, then rest for 5 minutes.

★ To serve, halve and lightly toast the bagels under the grill/broiler. Fill with lettuce, salmon sliders, onion pickles, crème fraîche and cornichons and serve at once.

BEEF & MOZZARELLA PEARL SLIDERS
with pesto mayo

THESE BEEF SLIDERS HAVE A DELIGHTFULLY GOOEY MOZZARELLA SURPRISE IN THE MIDDLE. THEY ARE GREAT FOR A PARTY OR AS PART OF A BUFFET – SIMPLY SCALE UP THE QUANTITIES.

200 g/7 oz. lean minced/ground beef

2 teaspoons tomato purée/paste

1 garlic clove, finely chopped

4 mozzarella pearls/bocconcini

a pinch of sea salt and freshly ground black pepper

to serve

4 mini ciabattas

Pesto Mayo (see page 129)

a handful of rocket/arugula leaves

makes 4

★ Preheat the oven to 180°C (350°F) Gas 4.

★ Put the beef in a bowl with the tomato purée/paste, garlic and salt and pepper. Work together with your hands until evenly mixed. Divide the beef mixture into four portions and shape into slider patties. Put a mozzarella pearl in the middle of each and then fold the beef mixture around it to reform the slider patties, with the mozzarella pearl hidden in the middle. Press each slider down to make them nice and flat.

★ Lay the sliders on a baking sheet and bake in the preheated oven for 20 minutes, turning halfway through cooking. When cooked, remove from the oven and let stand for 4 minutes before serving to allow the mozzarella to cool a little.

★ Slice the mini ciabattas in half and spread the bottom half of each with a little Pesto Mayo. Put a cooked slider on top and add a few rocket/arugula leaves. Finish the sliders with the lids of the mini ciabattas and serve at once.

BEEF, GOAT'S CHEESE & BEAN BURGER with pesto mayo

15 g/1 tablespoon butter

1 garlic clove, finely chopped

30 g/¼ cup shelled fresh broad/fava beans

160 g/6 oz. lean minced/ground beef

15 g/½ oz. goat's cheese, crumbled

4 teaspoons tomato purée/paste

1 tablespoon beaten egg

3 tablespoons fresh breadcrumbs

a pinch of sea salt and freshly ground black pepper

to serve

2 wholemeal/wholewheat bread rolls

butter, for spreading

Pesto Mayo (see page 129)

watercress and radish salad (optional)

serves 2

EATING FRESH BROAD/FAVA BEANS POPPED STRAIGHT OUT OF THEIR PODS IS A GREAT TREAT IF YOU ARE LUCKY ENOUGH TO GROW YOUR OWN, BUT MAKE SURE YOU SAVE SOME TO MAKE THESE DELICIOUS SUMMERTIME BURGERS.

★ Preheat the oven to 180°C (350°F) Gas 4.

★ Melt the butter in a frying pan/skillet set over a medium heat and add the garlic. Add the broad/fava beans and stir until browned. When cooked, remove from the pan, crush with a fork and set aside to cool.

★ Put the beef in a bowl with the goat's cheese, tomato purée/paste, egg, breadcrumbs and salt and pepper. Work together with your hands until evenly mixed. Add the crushed broad/fava beans and mix again. Divide the mixture in half and shape into two burger patties. Press each burger down to make them nice and flat. Lay the burgers on a baking sheet and bake in the preheated oven for 20 minutes, turning halfway through cooking.

★ Slice the bread rolls in half and spread both cut sides of each roll with a little butter. Put a cooked burger on the bottom half of each bread roll and top with a spoonful of pesto mayo. Finish the burgers with the lids of the bread rolls and serve with a watercress and radish salad, if liked.

BEEF, ROASTED RED PEPPER & LIME BURGER with crème fraîche & lamb's lettuce

LIGHT, BRIGHT AND TANGY, THIS UNUSUAL COMBINATION OF INGREDIENTS WORKS TOGETHER TO CREATE A TASTY SUMMERTIME BURGER. FOR A LIGHTER OPTION, SERVE THIS BURGER WITHOUT A BUN ON A BED OF CHOPPED LAMB'S LETTUCE.

½ red (bell) pepper, deseeded and chopped

2 tablespoons olive oil

200 g/7 oz. minced/ground beef

2 teaspoons paprika

freshly grated zest of ½ a lime

3 tablespoons fresh breadcrumbs

1 tablespoon beaten egg

1 garlic clove, finely chopped

a pinch of sea salt and freshly ground black pepper

to serve

2 seeded wholemeal/wholewheat bread rolls

a handful of lamb's lettuce/corn salad leaves, chopped

crème fraîche/sour cream

lime wedges, for squeezing

serves 2

★ Preheat the grill/broiler to high.

★ Drizzle the pepper pieces with the oil and sprinkle with salt and pepper. Put them on a baking sheet and cook under the grill/broiler for 8–10 minutes, shaking regularly to brown evenly. Remove from the grill/broiler and set aside to cool.

★ Put the beef in a bowl with the paprika, lime zest, breadcrumbs, egg, garlic and salt and pepper. Add the roasted pepper pieces and work together with your hands until evenly mixed. Divide the beef mixture in half and shape into two burger patties. Press each burger down to make them nice and flat.

★ Put the burgers on a baking sheet and grill/broil for 5 minutes on each side until cooked through.

★ Slice the bread rolls in half and put a few lamb's lettuce/corn salad leaves on the bottom half of each. Add the cooked burgers and top with a large spoonful of crème fraîche/sour cream. Finish the burgers with the lids of the bread rolls, if using, and serve at once with lime wedges, for squeezing.

BEEF, LEEK & MUSHROOM BURGER

with roasted root vegetables & mustard mayo

1 leek, finely chopped plus ½ a leek, roughly chopped

10 mushrooms, finely chopped

2 sprigs of fresh thyme, chopped

5 tablespoons olive oil

1 medium potato, peeled and chopped

1 sweet potato, peeled and chopped

½ butternut squash, peeled and chopped

1 carrot, peeled and chopped

1 red onion, roughly chopped

2 garlic cloves, finely chopped

1 sprig of fresh rosemary, chopped

420 g/15 oz. lean minced/ground beef

1½ tablespoons fresh breadcrumbs

sea salt and freshly ground black pepper

to serve

Mustard Mayo (see page 128)

mixed green vegetables of your choice, cooked (optional)

serves 4

THIS RECIPE TAKES COMFORT FOOD TO THE NEXT LEVEL, COMBINING SUCCULENT OVEN-ROASTED BURGERS WITH LOTS OF LOVELY WARMING WINTER VEGETABLES. WHAT MORE COULD YOU ASK FOR ON A COLD WINTER'S DAY?

★ Preheat the oven to 180°C (350°F) Gas 4.

★ Put the finely-chopped leek and mushrooms in a baking dish. Add the thyme and season with salt and pepper. Pour 3 tablespoons of the olive oil over the top and bake in the preheated oven for 15–20 minutes until soft and browned. When cooked, remove from the oven and set aside to cool. Leave the oven on.

★ Meanwhile, bring a large saucepan of water to the boil. Add the remaining ½ leek, potato, sweet potato, squash and carrot and boil for 5 minutes. Drain the vegetables and put them in a baking dish. Add the onion, garlic and rosemary and drizzle the remaining olive oil over the top. Mix to coat and bake in the oven for 20 minutes.

★ To make the burgers, put the beef in a bowl with the breadcrumbs and salt and pepper. Work together with your hands until evenly mixed. Add the leek and mushroom mixture and mix again. Divide the mixture into four portions and shape into burger patties. Press each burger down to make them nice and flat.

★ After baking the vegetables for 20 minutes, remove the dish from the oven and stir the vegetables to mix. Make small spaces between the vegetables and nestle the burgers in the gaps.

★ Return to the oven for 20–25 minutes, turning the burgers over halfway through cooking. Put a spoonful of Mustard Mayo on top of each burger and top each with two cooked green beans, if liked. Serve with mixed green vegetables of your choice.

PORK & ANTIPASTI BURGER

with lemon mayo

THIS LIGHT MEDITERRANEAN-STYLE BURGER BRINGS YOU ALL THE FLAVOURS OF AN ITALIAN ANTIPASTI SPREAD WITH EVERY MOUTHFUL. THESE ARE AT THEIR MOST DELICIOUS SERVED IN WARMED ROSEMARY FOCCACIA ROLLS.

½ red or yellow (bell) pepper, deseeded and diced

4 mushrooms, diced

70 g/⅔ cup diced aubergine/eggplant

80 g/¾ cup diced courgette/zucchini

2 tablespoons olive oil

140 g/5 oz. lean minced/ground pork

3 tablespoons fresh breadcrumbs

2 teaspoons tomato purée/paste

2 teaspoons fresh green or red pesto

1 garlic clove, crushed

a pinch of sea salt and freshly ground black pepper

to serve

2 rosemary foccacia rolls, warmed

Lemon Mayo (see page 129)

a handful of lettuce leaves

lemon wedges, for squeezing

serves 2

★ Preheat the oven to 180°C (350°F) Gas 4.

★ Put the pepper, mushrooms, aubergine/eggplant and courgette/zucchini in a baking dish with the olive oil and salt and pepper. Roast in the preheated oven for 25–30 minutes until soft and brown. Remove from the oven and set aside to cool. Leave the oven on.

★ Put the pork in a bowl with the breadcrumbs, tomato purée/paste, pesto, garlic and salt and pepper. Work together with your hands until evenly mixed. Add the cooled vegetables and mix again. Divide the mixture in half and shape into two burger patties. Press each burger down to make them nice and flat. Lay the burgers on a baking sheet and bake in the preheated oven for 25 minutes, turning halfway through cooking.

★ Cut the rolls in half and lightly toast under the grill/broiler or in the toaster. Spread a spoonful of Lemon Mayo on the base of each roll, add the lettuce leaves and top with the cooked burgers. Finish with the lids of the rosemary foccacia rolls and serve at once with lemon wedges for squeezing.

PORK & APPLE SLIDERS

in fried potato 'buns'

2 teaspoons butter

50 g/½ cup finely diced dessert or cooking apple

180 g/6 oz. really good pork mince/ground pork

2 teaspoons dried breadcrumbs

2 teaspoons tomato purée/paste

a pinch of freshly chopped parsley

salt and freshly ground black pepper

potato 'buns'

4 new potatoes

2 teaspoons butter

cocktail sticks/toothpicks

makes 4

SLIDERS ARE USUALLY SERVED IN MINI BREAD ROLLS, BUT THIS RECIPE TAKES IT TO ANOTHER LEVEL BY USING FRIED POTATO DISCS INSTEAD. OF COURSE YOU CAN USE EITHER DEPENDING ON WHAT YOU FANCY.

★ Heat the butter in a frying pan/skillet over a medium heat and fry the diced apple pieces for about 6 minutes until they brown and start to go sticky. Remove the apple from the pan and set on a plate to cool (you can chill a plate in the fridge before you start to help speed this up). Don't worry about washing up the pan as it will be used again.

★ Mix the pork with a pinch of salt, the breadcrumbs, tomato purée/paste and parsley really well in a bowl. Add the apple pieces once they've cooled a bit and mix. Divide the mixture in half and then in half again to get four even pieces. Shape into four slider patties. Press each slider down to make them nice and flat.

★ Meanwhile, for the potatoes, bring a pan of water to the boil. Leave the skins on the new potatoes and slice them approximately 1 cm/½ in. thick. You need two slices per slider, but make a few spares in case any break (and to nibble while the sliders are cooking later!) – perhaps make 12 slices to be on the safe side. Add the potato slices to the boiling water and parboil them for just 2 minutes to soften. Drain and set aside.

★ Heat the butter in the same frying pan/skillet from earlier over a medium heat and pick out the best-looking potato slices to fry with a good crack of black pepper. Fry well and then set aside on a wire rack or paper towel, with the slices not touching each other to keep them crispy.

★ Add the sliders to the same pan and fry for 3–4 minutes on each side, until cooked through.

★ Put a slider between two potato slices and use a cocktail stick/toothpick to keep everything together, then serve at once.

2 tablespoons olive oil

1 garlic clove, finely chopped

2 shallots, finely chopped

6 mushrooms, finely chopped

¾ teaspoon wholegrain mustard

2 teaspoons tomato purée/paste

1 sprig of fresh thyme, chopped

300 g/10 oz. lean minced/ground beef

a large pinch of sea salt and freshly ground black pepper

pastry rounds

50 g/3 tablespoons unsalted butter, chilled and cubed

120 g/1 scant cup plain/all-purpose flour, plus extra for rolling out

a large pinch of sea salt

a little milk, for brushing

to serve

a handful of lamb's lettuce/corn salad leaves

cooked peas

tomato chutney of your choice

a rolling pin

a 9-cm/3½-in. round cookie cutter

serves 2

BEEF WELLINGTON BURGER
in a shortcrust pastry 'bun'

ONE OF THE FANCIEST BEEF DISHES, BEEF WELLINGTON ALSO WORKS WELL IN BURGER FORM! THIS GOURMET DELIGHT, FLAVOURED WITH MUSTARD, MUSHROOMS AND SHALLOT, HAS PASTRY ROUNDS INSTEAD OF A BUN.

★ Preheat the oven to 180°C (350°F) Gas 4.

★ To make the pastry, put the butter, flour and salt in a mixing bowl and rub together with your fingertips until it has the texture of breadcrumbs. Add 3 tablespoons of warm water and mix together. Add 3 more tablespoons of water and mix again. If the pastry feels too dry, add a drop more water to bind but not too much. It should not feel sticky. Wrap the pastry in clingfilm/plastic wrap and chill it in the fridge while you make the burgers.

★ Heat half the oil in a frying pan/skillet set over a medium–high heat. Add the garlic, shallots and mushrooms and fry until soft and brown. Remove from the heat and add the wholegrain mustard, tomato purée/paste and thyme and mix well. Set aside to cool.

★ Remove the pastry from the fridge and roll out to a thickness of 1-cm/½-in. on a lightly-floured surface. Stamp out four pastry rounds using the cookie cutter.

★ Put the pastry rounds on a greased baking sheet and brush them with a little milk. Bake in the preheated oven for 15–20 minutes, until golden brown.

★ To make the burgers, put the beef in a bowl with the salt and pepper. Work together with your hands until evenly mixed. Add the shallot and mushroom mixture and mix again. Divide the mixture in half and shape into two burger patties. Press each burger down to make them nice and flat.

★ Heat the remaining oil in a frying pan/skillet and fry the burgers over a medium–high heat for 5–6 minutes on each side until cooked through.

★ When cooked, remove the pastry rounds from the oven and lay half of them face up. Top with the cooked burgers and some lettuce leaves. Cover with the remaining pastry rounds and serve with peas and tomato chutney on the side.

OLIVE, FETA & LAMB BURGER

500 g/1 lb. 2 oz. minced/ground lamb

60 g/4 tablespoons dried breadcrumbs

1 egg, beaten

50 g/½ cup pitted black olives, chopped

50 g/2 oz. feta cheese, crumbled

30 g/2 tablespoons tomato purée/paste

a big pinch of freshly chopped parsley

1 garlic clove, finely chopped

2 teaspoons olive oil, plus extra for frying

salt and freshly ground black pepper

to serve

4 pita breads

shredded cos/romaine lettuce

sour cream

lemon wedges

serves 4

LAMB COMBINES PERFECTLY WITH BLACK OLIVES AND FETA CHEESE, RESULTING IN JUICY BURGERS WHICH ARE STILL QUITE LIGHT AND FRESH-TASTING. PERFECT FOR SERVING IN THE SUMMER.

★ Mix all the ingredients, apart from those to serve, really well in a bowl, squeezing the mixture together to help it to bind. Divide the mixture into four portions and shape into burger patties. Press each burger down to make them nice and flat.

★ Heat a little olive oil in a frying pan/skillet over a high heat. Fry the burgers for 30 seconds on each side, then turn the heat down to medium and fry for a further 5 minutes on each side.

★ Lightly toast the pita breads under the grill/broiler or in the toaster, then split and fill them with shredded lettuce. Pop a burger into each pita pocket and add a spoonful of sour cream and a squeeze of fresh lemon juice. Season with salt and pepper to taste.

HERBY BURGER

with pineapple & avocado relish

OREGANO IS VERY EASY TO GROW – KEEP A POT ON YOUR KITCHEN WINDOWSILL AND YOU WILL HAVE A READY SUPPLY OF FRESH LEAVES. HERE IT COMBINES WITH GARLIC TO PRODUCE A HERBY BURGER WHICH IS SPICED UP WITH A SPOONFUL OF REFRESHING PINEAPPLE AND AVOCADO RELISH.

225 g/½ lb. lean minced/ground beef

2 teaspoons freshly chopped oregano

1 large garlic clove, crushed

sea salt and freshly ground black pepper

pineapple & avocado relish

75 g/2½ oz. fresh pineapple, peeled, cored and finely diced, or canned pineapple in natural juice

1 tablespoon freshly chopped mint

2 teaspoons freshly squeezed lemon juice

½ teaspoon dried chilli/red pepper flakes (optional)

½ small avocado, stoned, peeled and diced

to serve

2 seeded or plain wholegrain burger buns or rolls

2 lettuce leaves, such as cos/romaine or Little Gem

serves 2

★ Place the beef, oregano and garlic in a bowl. Season with salt and pepper, then work together with your hands until evenly mixed. Divide the mixture in half and shape into two burger patties. Press each burger down to make them nice and flat. Cover with clingfilm/plastic wrap and chill in the fridge for 30 minutes.

★ Preheat the grill/broiler to medium-high and line the grill pan with foil. Meanwhile, mix together the ingredients for the relish and set aside to allow the flavours to merge.

★ Grill/broil the burgers for 4–6 minutes on each side until cooked through.

★ Cut the buns in half and lightly toast under the grill/broiler. Put a lettuce leaf on each bottom half. Place the burgers on top and add a spoonful of the relish. Top with the second half of the burger bun and serve.

POTATO ROSTI BURGER

THIS MEAT-FREE RECIPE USES GRATED POTATOES TO CREATE A DELICIOUS ROSTI-STYLE BURGER. YOU WILL NEED TWO LARGE FRYING PANS/SKILLETS, OR YOU COULD USE AN OUTDOOR BARBECUE/GRILL.

200 g/7 oz. Maris Piper or other floury potatoes, peeled and grated

2 tablespoons plain/all-purpose flour

1 teaspoon sea salt, plus extra to season

a pinch of freshly ground black pepper

200 g/1¾ sticks butter

100 ml/⅓ cup vegetable oil

4 large Portobello mushrooms, stems removed

2 large beefsteak tomatoes, sliced

white sugar, to season

250 g/9 oz. halloumi cheese, sliced

100 g/3½ oz. Cheddar cheese, grated

Worcestershire sauce, to taste

to serve

4 large soft white rolls, sliced in half

1 cooked beetroot/beet, grated

Homemade Tomato Ketchup (see page 127)

leaves of 1 Little Gem lettuce

wooden skewers

serves 4

★ Put the grated potato in a bowl and add the flour, sea salt and a good pinch of black pepper. Stir to combine the ingredients until evenly mixed, then divide the potato mixture into four equal portions and shape into patties with the same diameter as the bread rolls. Ideally, they should be at least 5 mm/¼ in. thick.

★ Put the butter and vegetable oil in a large frying pan/skillet over a medium heat and heat until sizzling. Carefully place the potato patties in the pan and cook until they are just golden. Turn and repeat on the other side. Remove from the pan and set aside. Save the oil for later.

★ Lightly sprinkle the mushrooms with sea salt, gill-side up, and set aside. Sprinkle the tomato slices with a little sea salt and sugar.

★ Place the tomatoes and mushrooms in a large frying pan/skillet, baste the mushrooms in their cooking juices and cook gill-side down for a couple of minutes. Add the halloumi slices and potato patties (you will probably need to use a second pan/skillet) and continue cooking for a few minutes until the tomatoes and cheese are starting to colour. Turn everything over to cook the other side.

★ Moisten the rolls with the reserved potato cooking oil and place, oiled-side down, on a preheated ridged stovetop grill pan.

★ Sprinkle the Cheddar on top of the mushrooms and drizzle with a little Worcestershire sauce. Cover with a lid and cook for 5 minutes.

★ To assemble your burgers, put some grated beetroot/beet on the roll bases, followed by a mushroom with melted Cheddar, potato patty, a splash of Homemade Tomato Ketchup, 2 lettuce leaves, halloumi and tomato slices, topped with the bun. Use a wooden skewer to secure it all together.

SUPERFOOD BURGER

THESE ARE THE ULTIMATE FANCY SUPERFOOD BEEF BURGERS, CRAMMED WITH EXTRA GOOD STUFF LIKE IRON AND ANTIOXIDANTS AS WELL AS VITAMINS A, B6 AND C.

300 g/10½ oz. minced/ ground beef

1 cooked beetroot/beet, grated

½ cooking apple, peeled and diced

4 teaspoons tomato purée/paste

1 teaspoon powdered spirulina (optional)

4 teaspoons dried breadcrumbs (optional)

1 garlic clove, finely chopped

a pinch each of salt and freshly ground black pepper

vegetable oil, for frying

to serve

2 wholemeal/whole-wheat rolls

baby spinach leaves

hummus

serves 2

★ Mix the beef, grated beetroot/beet, diced cooking apple, tomato purée/paste, spirulina and breadcrumbs (if using), garlic, salt and pepper together with your hands until well mixed.

★ Divide the mixture in half and shape into two burger patties. Press each burger down to make them nice and flat.

★ Heat a little oil in a frying pan/skillet over a high heat and put the burgers in. Don't turn them too quickly; let them sear fully on the first side for 4–5 minutes before you move them. Turn and cook on the other side for 5–6 minutes, until they're cooked thoroughly in the middle.

★ Lightly toast the rolls under the grill/broiler. Add a layer of baby spinach leaves to the bottom halves, add the burgers and a dollop of hummus. Top with the remaining halves of the rolls and serve at once.

750 g/1½ lb. skinless boneless chicken breasts, minced/ground

2 garlic cloves, crushed

1 tablespoon freshly chopped rosemary

freshly grated zest and juice of 1 unwaxed lemon

1 egg yolk

50 g/⅓ cup dried breadcrumbs or matzo meal

1 medium aubergine/eggplant

2 courgettes/zucchini

sea salt and freshly ground black pepper

olive oil, for brushing

tapenade

125 g/⅔ cup black olives, pitted

2 anchovies in oil, drained

1 garlic clove, crushed

2 tablespoons capers, rinsed

1 teaspoon Dijon mustard

4 tablespoons extra virgin olive oil

to serve

4 slices of focaccia bread

radicchio or rocket/arugula leaves

serves 4

OPEN CHICKEN BURGER
with grilled vegetables

THIS OPEN-FACED BURGER IS FULL OF THE DELICIOUS FLAVOURS OF MEDITERRANEAN COOKING, WITH CHARGRILLED VEGETABLES, FOCACCIA BREAD AND SALTY OLIVE TAPENADE.

★ To make the tapenade, put the olives, anchovies, garlic, capers, mustard and oil in a food processor and blend to form a fairly smooth paste. Season to taste with pepper. Transfer to a dish, cover and store in the refrigerator for up to 5 days.

★ Put the chicken, garlic, rosemary, lemon zest and juice, egg yolk, breadcrumbs and some salt and pepper in a food processor and pulse until smooth. Transfer the mixture to a bowl, cover and chill for 30 minutes. Divide the mixture into four portions and shape into burger patties. Press each burger down to make them nice and flat.

★ Cut the aubergine/eggplant into 12 slices and the courgettes/zucchini into 12 thin strips. Brush with olive oil and season with salt and pepper. Barbecue or grill/broil the vegetables for 2–3 minutes on each side until charred and softened. Keep them warm.

★ Meanwhile, brush the chicken patties lightly with olive oil and barbecue or grill/broil for 5 minutes on each side until charred and cooked through. Keep them warm.

★ Toast the focaccia and top each slice with radicchio or rocket/arugula leaves, patties, grilled vegetables and some tapenade. Serve at once.

MACKEREL BURGER
with gooseberry sauce

THE OILINESS OF MACKEREL BALANCES WELL WITH A TART SAUCE AND A CLASSIC PARTNER IS GOOSEBERRY, ESPECIALLY AS THEY TEND TO COME INTO SEASON AS THE MACKEREL BECOMES PLENTIFUL. IF GOOSEBERRIES ARE OUT OF SEASON, THEN TRY THIS DISH WITH A HORSERADISH OR HOLLANDAISE SAUCE.

200 g/2 cups gooseberries, cut in half

70 g/⅓ cup caster/granulated sugar

100 g/7 tablespoons butter

4 whole mackerel (each about 170 g/6 oz.), filleted and deboned

4 brioche buns (or brioche finger rolls), sliced in half

80 g/1½ cups watercress

a pinch of salt and freshly ground black pepper

serves 4

★ Begin by making the sauce. Put the gooseberries in a small saucepan with the sugar and 100 ml/⅓ cup water set over a gentle heat. Cover and cook for about 15 minutes, until the gooseberries are soft. Blend the mixture using a handheld electric blender, then pour the liquid through a fine-mesh sieve/strainer into a jug/pitcher. Discard the pulp and store in the fridge.

★ Put the butter in a large frying pan/skillet set over a medium heat. When the butter is foaming, carefully add the mackerel fillets skin-side up and cook for 3–4 minutes, until cooked through.

★ To serve, place a small handful of watercress in each roll, then a generous dollop of gooseberry sauce and finally, two of the mackerel fillets. Season with salt and pepper to taste.

CHAPTER 8
SIDE ORDERS

ALE-BATTERED ONION RINGS

ONION RINGS AND FRENCH FRIES OFTEN COMPETE FOR THE TITLE OF MAIN SIDE DISH. ALTHOUGH FRENCH FRIES ARE MORE COMMON, IT ISN'T UNTIL YOU HAVE AN ONION RING IN YOUR MOUTH THAT YOU REALIZE THAT IF YOU WERE GIVEN THE OPTION, YOU WOULD EAT ONION RINGS FAR MORE OFTEN. THE BATTER USED TO COAT THE ONIONS INCLUDES INDIA PALE ALE (IPA) WHICH ADDS A LOVELY RICHNESS. THE ALCOHOL COOKS OFF WHEN THE ONIONS ARE FRIED.

120 g/1 cup plain/all-purpose flour, plus extra for dusting

250 ml/1 cup India pale ale

2 large brown or Vidalia onions

canola/rapeseed oil, for frying

salt, to taste

serves 4

★ Put the flour into a mixing bowl and make a well in the centre. Pour the ale into the well and whisk until combined. Let the mixture rest, covered, for 1 hour.

★ Peel the onions and cut crosswise into 1-cm/½-inch thick rings. Dust the rings with more flour, shaking off the excess, and coat them with the batter.

★ Heat 5 cm/2 inches of oil in a large frying pan/skillet. The pan is at the right temperature when the oil is steadily bubbling. Working in batches, fry the onion rings until they are golden in colour. Use a slotted spoon to transfer the onion rings onto paper towels to drain. Sprinkle them with salt to taste.

NEW MEXICO POTATO SALAD

A SIMPLE, TASTY AND INVENTIVE WAY OF USING THE FIRST POTATOES OF THE NEW SEASON. WITH AN ADDED KICK OF CHILLI/CHILE, THIS IS A GREAT ACCOMPANIMENT TO ANYTHING FROM THE BARBECUE/GRILL.

6 medium waxy potatoes, such as Ratte or Charlotte, scrubbed

1 tablespoon olive oil

1 tablespoon freshly squeezed lemon juice

4 UK large/US extra-large free-range eggs

4 large, mild green chillies/chiles, roughly chopped

5 large spring onions/scallions, chopped

200 g/scant cup Classic Mayo (see page 128)

sea salt and freshly ground black pepper

serves 4–6

★ Put the potatoes in a large saucepan of lightly salted boiling water, cover and bring back to the boil. Cook for 20–30 minutes until cooked but still firm. Drain and add the oil and lemon juice. Replace the lid and give them a good shake. Cool to room temperature with the lid on.

★ Boil the eggs in a small pan of salted water for 10 minutes. Remove from the heat and run the eggs under cold water. Shell them and let cool, then cut into medium-sized pieces.

★ Cut the potatoes into cubes and put in a large bowl with the chillies/chiles, spring onions/scallions and Classic Mayo. Mix well. Add the eggs and stir through very gently. Season to taste.

SWEET POTATO WEDGES

2 sweet potatoes, unpeeled, sliced into wedges

olive oil, for drizzling

sea salt and freshly ground black pepper

cajun spice rub (optional)

serves 2

THE ESSENTIAL MODERN ACCOMPANIMENT TO ANY VEGGIE BURGER IS THE SWEET POTATO WEDGE. YOU CAN KEEP THIS HEALTHY HOT SIDE COOKING IN THE OVEN WHILE THE GRILL/BROILER IS CROWDED WITH BURGERS, SKEWERS AND OTHER DELIGHTS.

★ Preheat the oven to 180°C (350°F) Gas 4.

★ Bring a large saucepan of water to the boil. Add the sweet potatoes and boil for about 5 minutes. Remove the potatoes from the pan and lay on a greased baking sheet.

★ Drizzle some olive oil over the top, sprinkle with black pepper and cajun spice rub, if using, and mix to coat.

★ Bake in the preheated oven for 25 minutes until brown and crisp. Shake the baking sheet frequently to make sure the wedges brown evenly without sticking.

★ Remove from the oven, sprinkle with salt and serve.

CLASSIC HOMECUT FRIES

THERE ARE SOME KIDS THAT WON'T EAT A BURGER WITHOUT CLASSIC HOMECUT FRIES, AND PROBABLY SOME ADULTS TOO! BAKING RATHER THAN DEEP-FRYING STILL GIVES GREAT FLAVOUR BUT IS SLIGHTLY HEALTHIER. SERVE WITH CLASSIC DIPS OF YOUR CHOOSING.

2 floury potatoes, sliced into fries

olive oil, for drizzling

sea salt and freshly ground black pepper

serves 2

★ Preheat the oven to 180°C (350°F) Gas 4.

★ Bring a large saucepan of water to the boil. Add the potatoes and boil for about 5 minutes. Remove from the pan and lay on a greased baking sheet.

★ Drizzle some olive oil over the top, sprinkle with salt and pepper to taste and mix to coat. Bake in the preheated oven for 25 minutes until golden and crisp.

★ Shake the baking sheet frequently to make sure the fries brown evenly without sticking.

★ Remove from the oven, sprinkle with salt and serve immediately.

HOT & SMOKY BARBECUE SAUCE

HOMEMADE SAUCES ARE TASTY AND SIMPLE TO MAKE. THEY WILL STORE WELL FOR UP TO 5 DAYS OR FOR SEVERAL WEEKS IN STERILIZED JARS IN THE FRIDGE.

★ Put all the ingredients in a saucepan, bring to the boil and simmer gently for 15 minutes until thickened and reduced. Season to taste with salt and pepper, then let cool completely.

★ Pour into a clean jar and store in the fridge for up to five days. If using sterilized jars, pour the hot sauce directly into the jar and when cold, seal and store in the fridge.

200 ml/¾ cup passata/strained tomatoes

100 ml/scant ½ cup maple syrup

50 ml/3 tablespoons black treacle/dark molasses

50 ml/3 tablespoons tomato ketchup, homemade (see recipe right) or store bought

50 ml/3 tablespoons white wine vinegar

2 tablespoons Worcestershire sauce

1 tablespoon hot chilli/chile sauce

2 teaspoons Dijon mustard

1 teaspoon garlic powder

1 teaspoon smoked paprika

sea salt and freshly ground black pepper

makes 350 ml/1½ cups

HOMEMADE TOMATO KETCHUP

GIVE THE STEADFAST KETCHUP FANS IN YOUR LIFE A REAL TREAT WITH THIS EASY RECIPE; IT IS SO MUCH BETTER THAN THE STORE-BOUGHT VERSION.

2 tablespoons olive oil

1 onion, finely chopped

2 garlic cloves, crushed

450 ml/2 scant cups passata/strained tomatoes

150 ml/⅔ cup red wine vinegar

150 g/¾ cup soft brown sugar

2 tablespoons black treacle/dark molasses

2 tablespoons tomato purée/paste

1 teaspoon Dijon mustard

2 bay leaves

1 teaspoon sea salt

½ teaspoon freshly ground black pepper

makes about 400 ml/1¾ cups

★ Heat the oil in a saucepan, add the onion and garlic and fry gently for 10 minutes until softened.

★ Add the remaining ingredients, bring to the boil, reduce the heat and simmer gently for 30 minutes until thickened and reduced by about one third.

★ Pass the sauce through a fine-mesh sieve/strainer, let cool and pour into a clean bottle and store in the fridge for up to five days. If using sterilized bottles, pour the hot sauce directly into the bottle and when cold, seal and store in the fridge.

CLASSIC MAYO

3 egg yolks

2 teaspoons Dijon mustard

2 teaspoons white wine vinegar or freshly squeezed lemon juice

½ teaspoon sea salt

300 ml/2 cups olive oil

makes about 400 ml/2 cups

★ Put the egg yolks, mustard, vinegar or lemon juice and salt in a food processor and blend until foaming. With the blade running, gradually pour in the oil through a funnel until thick and glossy. If it is too thick, add a little water. Adjust the seasoning to taste.

★ Spoon into a bowl and serve. Keeps well in the fridge for up to three days.

MUSTARD MAYO

1 recipe Classic Mayo

2 tablespoons wholegrain mustard

makes about 400 ml/2 cups

★ Make the Classic Mayo following the method in the recipe, left, but omitting the Dijon mustard. Transfer to a bowl and stir in the wholegrain mustard. Use as required or store as before in the fridge.

HERB MAYO

- - - - - - - - - - - - - - -

1 recipe Classic Mayo

a handful of any freshly chopped green herbs, such as basil, parsley or tarragon

makes about 400 ml/2 cups

★ Make the Classic Mayo following the method in the recipe, far left. Add the herbs to the food processor and blend until the sauce is speckled green. Use as required or store as before.

LEMON MAYO

- - - - - - - - - - - - - - -

1 recipe Classic Mayo

1 teaspoon freshly squeezed lemon juice

1 teaspoon finely grated lemon zest

a pinch of freshly ground black pepper

makes about 400 ml/2 cups

★ Make the Classic Mayo following the method in the recipe, far left, adding the lemon juice, zest and pepper with the mustard and vinegar. Blend until thickened. Use as required or store as before.

Variation: For a Lime Mayo, simply replace the lemon zest and juice with the zest and juice from a lime.

PESTO MAYO

- - - - - - - - - - - - - - -

1 recipe Classic Mayo

1 teaspoon green pesto

makes about 400 ml/2 cups

★ Make the Classic Mayo following the method in the recipe, far left, adding the pesto at the same time as the mustard and vinegar. Blend until thickened. Use as required or store as before.

CLASSIC COLESLAW

NO BURGER MEAL WITH ALL THE TRIMMINGS WOULD BE
COMPLETE WITHOUT A LARGE BOWL OF HOMEMADE COLESLAW.
YOU CAN ALTER THE PROPORTIONS OF VEGETABLES IF YOU WISH,
OR USE JUST WHITE CABBAGE RATHER THAN A MIXTURE OF
RED AND WHITE.

125 g/1 generous cup shredded
white cabbage

125 g/1 generous cup shredded
red cabbage

175 g/1½ cups grated carrots

½ white onion, thinly sliced

1 teaspoon sea salt, plus extra
for seasoning

2 teaspoons caster/superfine sugar

1 tablespoon white wine vinegar

50 ml/3½ tablespoons Classic Mayo
(see page 128)

50 ml/3 tablespoons single/light
cream

freshly ground black pepper

serves 4–6

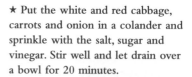

★ Put the white and red cabbage,
carrots and onion in a colander and
sprinkle with the salt, sugar and
vinegar. Stir well and let drain over
a bowl for 20 minutes.

★ Transfer the vegetables to a clean
kitchen cloth and squeeze out any
excess liquid. Put them in a large
bowl and stir in the Classic Mayo
and cream. Season to taste with salt
and pepper and serve.

SOUR CREAM SLAW

BECAUSE OF ITS TANGY, FRESH TASTE, NOTHING GOES WITH WARM WEATHER LIKE HOMEMADE COLESLAW. IT'S A GREAT COMPONENT FOR A PARTY WITH FRIENDS OR A FAMILY GET-TOGETHER.

1 celery stick, grated

80 g/⅔ cup grated green cabbage

1 carrot, grated

½ red onion (or 3 spring onions/scallions), finely chopped

1 teaspoon wholegrain mustard

1 tablespoon white wine vinegar

1 teaspoon dark brown sugar

100 ml/scant ½ cup sour cream

sea salt and freshly ground black pepper

serves 4

★ Put the celery, cabbage, carrot and onion in a large bowl. Stir in the mustard, white wine vinegar, sugar and sour cream. Season to taste with salt and pepper and serve.

HOME PICKLED CUCUMBER

1 pickling cucumber (e.g. ridge cucumber or gherkin)

3 tablespoons sea salt

200 ml/generous ¾ cup water

1 garlic clove, chopped

1 shallot, chopped

a pinch of freshly ground black pepper

2 bay leaves

a pinch of ground cinnamon

3 tablespoons distilled white vinegar

makes 1 jar (about 200 g/7 oz.)

THE WORLD OF CURING, PRESERVING AND FERMENTING IS FASCINATING – FROM SUSHI TO SALT BEEF, IT EXISTS IN ALMOST EVERY CUISINE OF THE WORLD. IT'S IN THE ACCOMPANIMENTS TOO, LIKE THIS RECIPE FOR CURING CUCUMBER OR GHERKINS AT HOME.

★ Slice the cucumber either crossways or lengthways and lay it on a plate. Sprinkle 1 tablespoon salt over the top and leave for 1 hour, to draw out a lot of the moisture.

★ Rinse the cucumber slices and pat dry with paper towels. Sterilize a jar, then put the cucumber slices into the jar.

★ Put the water and remaining salt into a saucepan and bring to the boil to make a brine. Remove from the heat and let cool a little, so it's not boiling hot.

★ Add the garlic, shallot, pepper, bay leaves and cinnamon to the jar, and shake. Add the vinegar, then pour the brine over the top.

★ Seal the lid and leave in the refrigerator for 2–3 days, before serving. Store in the fridge for up to 1 month.

CARAMELIZED RED ONIONS

- -

SWEETLY CARAMELIZED WITH HONEY, THESE RED ONIONS ARE VERY MOREISH AND MAKE A GREAT ACCOMPANIMENT TO BURGERS AND SLIDERS OF ALL TYPES.

1 red onion, thinly sliced

2 tablespoons runny honey

serves 2

★ Preheat the oven to 180°C (350°F) Gas 4.

★ Put the onion in an ovenproof dish (see Note), drizzle over the honey and stir to mix so that the onions are well coated.

★ Roast in the preheated oven for about 15 minutes, until caramelized. Roast for longer if you want them chewy and crispy. If you're doing a bigger batch, it's worth giving them a good shake halfway through the cooking time so that they all get a chance to caramelize.

★ You can freeze this in portions for 6 months, or it will keep in the fridge in a sealed container for up to 2 weeks.

Note: These caramelized onions get very sticky, so you may wish to line the ovenproof dish with foil, with the edges folded in, so that you can throw it away, rather than scrub sticky onions off the dish.

ROASTED PEPPER & CARAMELIZED ONION RELISH

2 ripe Romano-style red sweet/ bell peppers

2 tablespoons sunflower oil

1 large onion, diced

2 garlic cloves, crushed

2 tablespoons cider vinegar

1 tablespoon red wine vinegar

2 tablespoons brown sugar

2–3 red Jalapeño chillies/chiles (or other red chillies/chiles), chopped

1 tablespoon tomato purée/paste

2 teaspoons Cajun spice blend

½ teaspoon paprika

makes 1 jar (about 200 g/7 oz.)

RATHER THAN USING THE CONVENTIONAL TOMATO BASE, THIS RELISH USES ROASTED SWEET PEPPERS, WHOSE NATURAL SWEETNESS BALANCES VERY WELL WITH THE ACIDITY OF THE VINEGAR. THE RESULT IS SWEET, SOUR AND SPICY – PERFECT WITH SLIGHTLY SMOKY BURGERS. FOR A HOT, SMOKY RELISH, REDUCE THE FRESH CHILLI CONTENT AND ADD A GENEROUS TEASPOON OF CRUSHED CHIPOTLE CHILLI/CHILE.

★ Place the peppers on a baking sheet and put under a hot grill/broiler. When the skin has blackened on top, turn them over and repeat the process. Once all the skin is charred, turn off the grill/broiler and put the peppers into a medium food bag. Seal the top and set aside to cool.

★ When cool, peel the charred skins away from the flesh and deseed the peppers. Roughly dice the roasted pepper flesh.

★ Heat the oil in a medium heavy-based saucepan over a medium-high heat and fry the onion for 10–15 minutes, or until gradually caramelized. Stir frequently to prevent it from burning. When it has a nice golden colour, add the garlic and fry for 30–60 seconds, or until softened and golden. Add the peppers, both types of vinegar and the sugar. Bring to the boil, stirring constantly to dissolve the sugar (you can add a splash of water if needed). Reduce the heat and stir in the chillies/chiles, tomato purée/paste, Cajun spice and paprika. Add 100 ml/scant ½ cup water and return to a simmer. Cook for 10–15 minutes, stirring regularly and adding a little more water if required, until rich and thick. Adding little and often, and only if really needed, is best, as you want the end relish to be rich, thick and sticky.

★ Pour straight into a sterilized jar and seal. Leave to cool. Store in the fridge once opened.

ROCKET/ARUGULA, RADICCHIO & CRISPY BACON SALAD

YOU CAN USE ROCKET/ARUGULA ON ITS OWN IF YOU LIKE – JUST INCREASE TO 3 BUNDLES.

175 g/6 slices of smoked bacon
1 garlic clove, peeled but left whole
2 bundles of large rocket/arugula leaves
1 radicchio, torn into bite-sized pieces
50 g/½ cup pine nuts, toasted in a dry frying pan/skillet

dressing
3 tablespoons extra virgin olive oil
1 tablespoon freshly squeezed lemon juice
sea salt and freshly ground black pepper

serves 4

★ Heat a frying pan/skillet until hot, add the bacon and dry-fry for 2–3 minutes on each side until golden. Let cool and break into small pieces.

★ Rub the inside of a large salad bowl with the garlic clove. Wash the rocket/arugula and radicchio and dry in a salad spinner. Transfer to the bowl and add the bacon pieces and pine nuts.

★ Put all the dressing ingredients in a small bowl and whisk well. Sprinkle the dressing over the salad, toss gently to coat the leaves evenly and serve at once.

BABY LETTUCE SALAD
with creamy herb dressing

THIS SALAD HAS A LOVELY, TANGY, CREAMY DRESSING AND YOU CAN VARY THE FLAVOUR BY USING DIFFERENT HERBS, SUCH AS CHIVES OR MINT.

4 baby lettuces, such as Little Gem

dressing
4 tablespoons extra virgin olive oil
2 tablespoons sour cream
1 tablespoon white wine vinegar
¼ teaspoon caster sugar
2 spring onions/scallions, trimmed and finely chopped
1 tablespoon finely chopped fresh herbs, such as tarragon, basil and parsley
sea salt and freshly ground black pepper

serves 4

★ Separate the lettuce leaves. Wash them, dry them in a salad spinner or on kitchen paper and put them in a large salad bowl.

★ Put all the dressing ingredients in a small bowl and whisk until smooth. Season to taste with salt and pepper. Sprinkle the dressing over the lettuce, toss gently to coat the leaves evenly and serve at once.

ELOTES

THIS MEXICAN STREET FOOD PAIRS WELL WITH MANY OF THE BURGER AND SLIDER RECIPES IN THIS BOOK. COTIJA IS A HARD, CRUMBLY MEXICAN CHEESE, BUT PARMESAN OR RICOTTA WORK JUST AS WELL.

vegetable oil, for brushing

1 teaspoon chilli/chili powder

½ teaspoon cayenne pepper

8 corn on the cob/ears of corn

50 g/¼ cup mayonnaise or unsalted butter

40 g/½ cup crumbled Cotija, Parmesan or ricotta salata cheese

1 lime, cut into 8 wedges

serves 8

★ Build a medium-hot fire in a charcoal grill or preheat a grill/broiler to medium-high and brush the grill rack with oil.

★ Combine the chilli/chili powder and cayenne pepper in a small bowl.

★ Grill/broil the corn for about 10 minutes, turning occasionally with tongs, until cooked through and lightly charred. Remove from the grill and brush each ear with 1½ teaspoons of mayonnaise or butter. Sprinkle each with a tablespoon of cheese and a pinch of the chilli-cayenne mixture. Squeeze a lime wedge over each corn on the cob/ear of corn and serve.

★ Alternatively, remove the corn kernels from the cob after taking them off the grill, and combine the corn with the mayonnaise or butter and the cheese. Top with the chilli-cayenne mixture and a dash of lime juice.

CREAMED CORN & BACON

CREAMED CORN IS A RECIPE THAT MOST OF US ASSOCIATE WITH AN OLDER GENERATION, BUT LIKE MANY CLASSIC RECIPES, IT STAYS EXCITING WITH CONSTANT RE-INVENTION. HIGH SUMMER IS THE BEST TIME FOR THIS DISH, AS CORN IS AT ITS PEAK THEN.

6 corn on the cob/ears of corn

2 tablespoons olive oil

6 slices of bacon, cooked and roughly chopped

4 tablespoons salted butter

2 tablespoons plain/all-purpose flour

(UK) 60 ml double cream and 60 ml whole milk, mixed, or (US) ½ cup half and half

2 tablespoons freshly chopped coriander/cilantro, plus extra to garnish

salt and freshly ground black pepper

serves 4–6

★ Remove the corn from the cobs and set aside.

★ Heat the olive oil in a medium-sized frying pan/skillet and add the bacon when the oil is hot. Turn the bacon slices after a couple of minutes and continue cooking until they've crisped up a bit. Place them on paper towels to soak up the grease. Allow them to cool before chopping, and set aside.

★ In a medium saucepan melt the butter over a low heat. Whisk in the flour and then quickly whisk in the cream and milk, or half and half, a little at a time so that no clumps form. Stir in the bacon, corn, and coriander/cilantro. Taste and season with salt and pepper, as desired. Allow the mixture to simmer for a few minutes before removing from the heat.

★ Divide the corn mixture onto serving plates and garnish with more coriander/cilantro.

STRAWBERRY MILKSHAKE

THIS QUANTITY IS ENOUGH TO MAKE 2 LARGE OR 4 SMALL SERVINGS.

500 g/1 lb. 2 oz. strawberries, hulled

200 ml/1 cup cold milk

150 g/3 small scoops vanilla ice cream, plus extra to serve (optional)

strawberry syrup, to serve

serves 2–4

★ Put the strawberries, milk and ice cream in a blender and purée until smooth.

★ Trickle a little strawberry syrup down the inside of each glass, then pour in the smoothie. Serve at once with an extra scoop of ice cream on top, if using.

ICED COFFEE SHAKE

THIS IS A WONDERFULLY CREAMY ICED COFFEE THAT CAN BE TURNED INTO A DELICIOUS COCKTAIL BY ADDING JUST A DASH OF TÍA MARIA.

300 g/10 oz. vanilla ice cream, plus extra to serve (optional)

300 ml/1¼ cups cold milk

300 ml/1¼ cups iced espresso coffee

2 tablespoons Tía Maria (optional)

freshly grated chocolate, to serve

serves 4

★ Put the ice cream, milk, coffee and Tía Maria, if using, in a blender and purée until smooth.

★ Pour into 4 chilled glasses and serve topped with an extra scoop of ice cream, if using, and a dusting of grated chocolate.

INDEX

RECIPE CREDITS

Amy Ruth Finegold
Quinoa burgers with Portobello mushrooms

Carol Hilker
Ale-battered onion rings
Burnt ends burger
Creamed corn & bacon
Diner cheeseburger
Elotes
Pulled pork pretzel bun burger
Secret-sauce sliders

Dan May
Chilli veggie burger with sun-dried tomatoes
New Mexico potato salad
Roasted pepper and caramelized red onion relish

Dunja Gulin
Spicy vegan burgers

Jenny Linford
Roast garlic pork burger

Jordan Bourke
Beetroot/beets burger with wholegrain mustard mayonnaise

Louise Pickford
Baby lettuce salad with creamy herb dressing
Bacon burger with sour cream slaw
Barbecue burger with crispy onion rings
Buffalo cauliflower burger with blue cheese sauce
Cajun salmon, dill & crème fraîche sliders
Chicken burger with herb mayonnaise
Chicken steak & bacon burger with Caesar dressing
Chinese crispy duck sliders with hoisin & spring onions/scallions
Classic all-American hamburger
Classic Cheeseburger
Courgette/zucchini sliders with crispy kale, pesto & whipped feta
Creole spiced chicken burger
Deep-fried buttermilk chicken burger with 'nduja & slaw
Hawaiian teriyaki pork burger with pineapple rings & avocado mayonnaise

Healthy cod burger with watercress & almond pesto
Iced coffee shake
Jamaican jerk tuna burger with Tabasco mayonnaise
Japanese salmon katsu sliders
Malaysian prawn/shrimp sambal sliders
Mediterranean lamb burger
Middle Eastern sliders with tahini sauce
Mushroom burgers with chilli/chile mayonnaise & onion pickle
Open chicken burger with grilled vegetables
Open tex-mex burger with chilli/chile relish
Rocket/arugula, radicchio & crispy bacon salad
'Sausage' burgers for kids
Spiced pork burger with satay sauce
Sticky sweet chilli/chile halloumi sliders with crispy onion rings
Strawberry milkshake
Thai chicken breast burger with mango, crispy shallots & sweet chilli/chile dressing
Triple whammy brunch burger
Turkey burger with onion & cranberry jam/relish
Vietnamese sesame tofu banh mi burger with pickles

Lyndel Costain and Nicola Graimes
Herby burger with pineapple & avocado relish

Mat Follas
Mackerel burger with gooseberry sauce
Potato rosti burger

Miranda Ballard
Beef & black bean sliders with corn & pepper salsa
Beef & mozzarella pearl sliders with pesto mayo
Beef wellington burger in a shortcrust pastry 'bun'
Beef, goat's cheese & bean burger with pesto mayo
Beef, leek & mushroom burger with roasted root vegetables & mustard mayo
Beef, roasted red pepper & lime burger with crème fraîche & lamb's lettuce
Big breakfast burger with mushroom & fried egg
Caramelized red onions
Cheesy root vegetable burgers with mustard mayo
Chicken Caesar sliders wrapped in Parma ham
Chilli con carne burger wrapped in grilled courgette/zucchini slices
Christmas canapé sliders with cranberry sauce & Camembert
Chunky aubergine/eggplant burgers with pesto dressing
Classic beef burger with tomato ketchup & lettuce
Classic coleslaw
Classic homecut fries
Classic mayo
Curried sweet potato burgers
Fish burger with capers & tartare sauce
Garlic mushroom burger with caramelized aïoli
Herb mayo
Home pickled cucumber
Homemade tomato ketchup
Honey apple pork sliders with caramelized apple slices
Hot & smoky barbecue sauce
Indian-style lamb sliders with minted yogurt & mango chutney
Italian burger with olives, sun-dried tomatoes & pesto
Lamb & feta burger with tzatziki, baby spinach & beetroot/beets
Lamb & mint sliders with roast potatoes & watercress
Lemon mayo
Mexican burger with sour cream, salsa & guacamole
Mustard mayo
Olive, feta & lamb burger
Open tofu bean burger
Pesto mayo
Pork & antipasti burger with lemon mayo
Pork & apple sliders in fried potato 'buns'
Pork & cider burger with blue cheese & asparagus
Sour cream slaw
Spanish chorizo & bean burger
Spiced falafel burger with tahini yogurt sauce
Spicy beef & pork sliders with ginger & lime
Superfood burger
Sweet potato wedges
Ultimate bacon-cheese burger with tomato relish

Rachael Anne Hill
Rice & bean burgers

Rose Hammick and Charlotte Packer
Surprise burger

Shelagh Ryan
Spicy pork burger with mango salsa

Ryland Peters & Small
Mini party hamburgers

PICTURE CREDITS